Learning th
Tabla
Vol. 2
by David Courtney

Online Audio   www.melbay.com/20871BCDEB

Audio contents

1	Mukhada in Tintal
2	Exercise (Example 2)
3	Exercise (Example 3)
4	Exercise (Example 4)
5	Exercise (Example 5)
6	Exercise (Example 6)
7	Exercise (Example 7)
8	Mukhada in FastTintal
9	Mukhada in Tintal
10	Mukhada in Tintal
11	Mukhada in Tintal
12	Mukhada in Jhaptal
13	Tukada in Tintal
14	Tukada in Tintal
15	Tukada in Tintal
16	Tukada in Tintal
17	Exercise (Example 17)
18	Benchmark Test (Example 18)
19	Benchmark Test (Example 19)
20	Benchmark Test (Example 20)
21	Exercise (Example 21)
22	Exercise (Example 22)
23	Exercise (Example 13)
24	Exercise (Example 24)
25	Exercise (Example 25)
26	Exercise (Example 26)
27	Exercise (Example 27)
28	Fast Tintal Prakar
29	Fast Dadra Prakar
30	Beginner's Practice Rela #1
31	Beginner's Practice Rela #2
32	Kaida/Rela in Tintal
33	Swatantra Rela in Jhaptal
34	Delhi Baj Kaida in Tintal
35	Exercise (Example 35)
36	Mukhada in Tintal
37	Exercise (Example 37)
38	Mukhada in Tintal
39	Simple Mukhada in Tintal
40	Exercise (Example 40)
41	Exercise (Example 41)
42	Exercise (Example 42)
43	Paran in Tintal
44	Tivra Tal
45	Chautal
46	Sool Tal
47	Dhammar Tal
48	Ultra-Fast TIntal Prakar
49	Ultra-Fast TIntal Prakar
50	Dadra Tal Prakar
51	Jhaptal Prakar
52	Rupak Tal Prakar
53	Dipchandi Prakar
54	Kaherava Prakar (Bhajan ka Theka)
55	Kaherava Filmi Prakar
56	Tilwada Tal
57	Jhoomra Tal
58	Exercise (Example 58)
59	Exercise (Example 59)
60	Exercise (Example 60)
61	Exercise (Example 61)
62	Damdar Tihai in Tintal
63	Damdar Tihai in Tintal
64	Damdar Tihai in Tintal
65	Damdar Tihai in Tintal
66	Damdar Tihai in Tintal
67	Bedam Tihai in Tintal
68	Bedam Tihai in Rupak Tal
69	Chakradar in Tintal
70	Gat in Tintal
71	Laggi in Kaherava

2 3 4 5 6 7 8 9 0

Visit us on the Web at www.melbay.com — E-mail us at email@melbay.com

CONTENTS

Preface 5

Introduction 6
   The Tabla 6
   Tal 6
   Bols 7
   Bols of the Right Hand 7
   Bols of the Left Hand..7
   Bols That Use Both Hands...8
   Bols Expressions 9
   Bols Which Have No Technique 9
   Notation 9
   Compositional Forms 10
   Overview of Defining Criteria for Compositions 11
   Linguistic Diversity 12
   Gharana 12
   Left-handedness 13
   Gender 13

More Bols 14
   Variations in Bols 14
   Complementary Forms 14
   New Bols and Technique 14

Mukhada and Tukada 18
   Mukhada...18
   Tukada 20

New Techniques for Familiar Bols 22
   Dhin 22
   TiTa 23
   TiRaKiTa 25
   Taa - TiTaKiRaNaaKa & Dhaa - TiTaGiRiNaaGa 26
   TiRaTiRaKiRaNaaKa & DhiRaDhiRaGiRaNaaGa...................................27
   Fast Prakars 28

Rela 31
   Structure of Rela 32
   Kaida-Rela 32
   Swatantra Rela 37

Another Kaida 39

Pakhawaj Material 43
    Pakhawaj vs. Tabla 43
    Gender Association 43
    New Bols 44
    Overview of Technique and Bols of Pakhawaj 47
    Compositional Forms 47
    Paran 47
    New Tals 48

More Tals and Prakars 50
    Ultra-Fast Tintal Prakar 50
    Dadra Prakar 50
    Jhaptal Prakar 51
    Rupak Prakar 51
    Dipchandi Prakar 51
    Kaherava Prakars 52
    Tilwada 52
    Jhoomra 53

Transitions 54
    TiRaKiTaTaKa 54
    TiTaKaTaGaDeeGeNa 55

More Tihais and Chakradars 58
    Tihai 58
    Chakradar 61

Gat 62

Laggi 64

Conclusion 67

Appendix 69

About the Authors 70

Figures

Tabla 7
Ga (two-fingered) 9
Ta, Ra 9
Ti 9
Tak or Kat 9
Tee 9
Tun, Tu, Too, Toon 9
Naa or Taa 10
Tin 10
Na, Ta, or Ra 10
Ga (one-fingered) 10
Ka or Kat 10
Dhin 10

PREFACE

This book/audio set is the sequel to "Learning the Tabla". The first set has been on the market for a few years. I have been heartened by the e-mails that I have received. Your numerous questions and comments about the previous set have been very helpful for me. I am pleased to be able to present this next set to you, which I trust will address many of your questions.

This set picks up where the last one left off. If by any chance you do not have the first one, I strongly recommend that you purchase it. There will be frequent references to its material.

The profile of the typical user was considered when putting this together. Some of you are Indian, so it is pointless to explain to you the cultural elements; yet many of you are non-Indian; therefore, such explanations are important. Many of you have teachers, but many of you are forced to learn on your own. Some of you really want to get every detail that can possibly be given; however, others may wish to just get down to the "licks" and forget all of the other stuff.

Whenever I am faced with these decisions, I am guided by a simple principle. I will generally lean toward giving too much information rather than giving too little. It is easy to skim through sections that are not interesting to you; however, it is very difficult to hunt for information that is not present.

A few words are in order concerning ones training. There is a very formalized approach to the learning of tabla that is based upon a time honoured relationship between teacher and student. This has been carefully considered when putting this set together. This set is intended to act as a supplement to the training that one is receiving under the teacher. As such, it provides alternative techniques, viewpoints, and approaches to the subject that the student otherwise might not encounter. Where the personal instruction is best at providing in-depth instruction, this set is designed to provide breadth in instruction. When this is used with the guidance of a teacher, it is an unbeatable combination.

However, I am not blind to the fact that many of you have no access to an instructor. Therefore, this set is self-explanatory; in a pinch it can stand alone.

There are a number of people who have made this work possible. First, I would like to thank my teachers, the late Ustad Shaik Dawood Khan of Hyderabad, and my pakhawaj teacher Ustad Zakir Hussain. I would also like to thank several other people who encouraged my early interest in Indian music. Specifically, I would like to thank Dr. Jayant Kirtane and K. S. Kalsi. Of course I would be remiss if I did not thank Mr. William Bay and all the people at Mel Bay Publications. There are also the people who have helped me proof-read the book; specifically I would like to thank Masood Raoofi, Gary Salamone, Rashida Parmer, Siraj Parmer, Tom Skelly, T.V. Natarajan, and Azmine Nimji for their suggestions. Finally, I must thank my wife Chandrakantha, for her patience and assistance. Without these people, this work would not be possible.

David Courtney
July 15, 2004
david@chandrakantha.com

INTRODUCTION

Let us start this volume by doing several things. First, we need to recap some of the important points from the first book/audio set; these form the foundation upon which this present work is based. We will also familiarize our-selves with a few conventions that we will be using in the rest of this volume. We will also look at the overall philosophy behind the various compositional forms. Finally, we will look at miscellaneous topics that need to be kept in mind when going through this work.

THE TABLA

The tabla is one of the most popular drums of India. Fifty years ago, it was largely unknown outside South Asia. In the last few decades, it has spread beyond its homeland to occupy a firm position in popular music, fusion, and world music.

Figure 1. Tabla

The tabla consists of a pair of drums (figure 1). The smaller wooden drum is known as the dayan, and is usually played with the right hand. The larger drum is made of metal; this is known as the bayan, and it is usually played with the left hand. Both drums are played together to produce a wide variety of compositions and improvisations in Indian music.

TAL

Indian music is based upon an abstract system of rhythm known as "tal". The word "tal" literally means "clapping of hands".

North Indian tals are based upon three different levels of structure. The most fundamental unit is the beat; this is known as the matra. The next unit is the measure; this is known as the vibhag. The larger and most important unit is the cycle; this is known as the avartan.

The measures (vibhags) are noteworthy in that they refer back to an ancient system of timekeeping. In this system, each vibhag is designated with either a clap or a wave of the hands. The clap is known as "tali", while the wave of the hands is referred to as "khali". The first clap of the cycle is especially significant; this is known as the "sam", and it represents a type of cadence found in Indian music.

The previous work introduced a number of tals. These are listed below:

Tintal - Tintal is a very common rhythm of 16 beats. It is divided into four measures (vibhags), of four beats (matras) each. All of the vibhags are clapped except for the third one, which is waved.

Jhaptal - Jhaptal is a very common rhythm of 10 beats. It is divided into four measures (vibhags). The first vibhag has two beats (matras), and is signified by a clap of the hands. The second vibhag has three beats, and is signified by a clap of the hands. The third vibhag has two beats, and is signified by a wave of the hand. The final vibhag has three beats, and is signified by a clap.

Dadra Tal - Dadra tal is a six beat tal commonly used in the lighter forms of music. It is composed of two vibhags of three beats each. The first vibhag is signified by a clap, and the second vibhag is signified by a wave of the hand.

Rupak Tal - Rupak tal has seven beats divided into three vibhags. The first vibhag is three beats and is signified by a wave. The second and third vibhags are of two beats each, and are both clapped. Rupak is noteworthy because it is the only tal that begins with a khali vibhag.

Dipchandi tal - Dipchandi is a tal of 14 beats. It is divided into four vibhags; all vibhags are clapped except for the third vibhag, which is signified by a wave. The vibhags are divided three, four, three, and four beats respectively.

Kaherava Tal - Kaherava is a tal of eight matras, and is commonly found in the lighter forms of music. It is divided into two vibhags of four beats each. The first vibhag is clapped, while the second vibhag is waved.

Ektal - Ektal is composed of 12 beats, divided into six vibhags of two beats each. The second and the fourth vibhag are waved while all of the others are clapped.

BOLS

Tabla training is based upon a series of mnemonic syllables. These syllables, known as "bol", represent the various strokes of the instrument. These bols may involve the left hand, the right hand or a combination of both. Furthermore, one finds bol expressions which may have a single identity but may encompass a string of strokes.

BOLS OF THE RIGHT HAND

Here is a list of bols of the right hand that were introduced in the first volume:

Naa(ना) - Naa is a sharp, rim-stroke on the dayan (figure 2).

Tin(तिं) - Tin is a soft, resonant stroke on the dayan (figure 3).

Na(न) - Na is a dull, nonresonant stroke on the dayan. It is played with the last two fingers of the right hand (figure 4).

Kat(कत्) - Kat(कत्) is usually a stroke on the bayan, but occasionally Kat(कत्) is a nonresonant stroke on the dayan (figure 5). Again, the context will usually indicate which technique is to be played.

Tee(ती) - Tee(ती) may be played different ways depending upon the context of the composition. Sometimes Tee(ती) is the same as Tin(तिं) (figure 3); however, it is often a nonresonant stroke of the dayan (figure 6).

Too(तू), Tu(तु), Tun(तुं), or **Toon(तूं)** - This is an open, resonant stroke of the right hand (figure 7).

Taa(ता) - This is one of the most fundamental strokes of the tabla. There are two common forms; there is a Purbi and there is a Delhi style. The Delhi style uses the same rim stroke as found for Naa(ना) (figure 2). Therefore, in most cases Naa(ना) and Taa(ता) are synonymous. However, there is also a Purbi style (figure 15). In this technique, it is played in the maidan in a fashion somewhat similar to Tin(तिं). However, it is much stronger than Tin(तिं).

BOLS OF THE LEFT HAND

Here is a list of bols of the left hand that were introduced in the first volume:

Ga(ग) - Ga is a resonant stroke of the bayan. Usually, it is played with the ring finger and middle finger of the left hand (figure 10); but sometimes it is played with just the index finger (figure 11).

Ka(क), Ke(के), Kat(कत्), or **Kin(किं)** - These are different names for the same stroke. This stroke is a nonresonant slap against the bayan (figure 12).

BOLS THAT USE BOTH HANDS

Here is a list of bols that use both the left and right hands; these were introduced in the first volume:

Dhee(धी) - This stroke may be executed in several ways. Sometimes it is synonymous with Dhin(धिं) (figure 13), sometimes this is a combination of Toon(तूं)(figure 7) and Ga(ग)(figure 10). There are other techniques which will be introduced in this volume.

Dhin(धिं) - Dhin is a combination of Tin(तिं) and Ga(ग) (figure 13).

Dhaa(धा) - Dhaa is a combination of Ga(ग) and Taa(ता)(figure 14).

Figure 2. Naa(ना) or Taa(ता) (Delhi Style)

Figure 3. Tin (तिं) (Delhi style)

Figure 4. Na(न), Ta(ट), Ra(ड)

Figure 5. Tak(तक), Kat(कत) (Purbi)

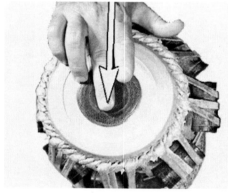

Figure 6. Tee (ती)

Figure 7. Tun(तूं)

Figure 8. Ta(ट), Ra(र)

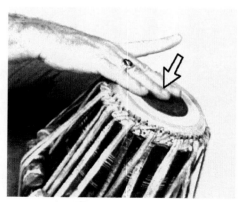

Figure 9. Ti(ति)

Figure 10. Ga(ग) (two finger)

8

Figure 11. Ga(ग) (one finger)

Figure 12. Ka(क), or Kat(कत)

Figure 13. Dhin(धिं)

Figure 14. Dhaa(धा) (Dilli-a.k.a Delhi Style)

Figure 15. Taa(ता) (purbi)

BOLS EXPRESSIONS

Here is a list of bol expressions that were introduced in the first volume:

TiTa (ति ट) - TiTa (ति ट) is a bol expression of the right hand composed of two nonresonant strokes. Its technique varies greatly. One common technique is to lead off with the middle finger (figure 6) followed by the index finger (figure 8). One other technique leads with the last three fingers (figure 9), and finishes with the index finger (figure 8).

TiRaKiTa (ति र कि ट) - TiRaKiTa is a bol expression composed of nonresonant strokes of both hands. There are numerous techniques used to execute this stroke.

Taa - TiTaKiRaNaaKa (ता - ति ट कि ड ना क) - This is a bol expression composed of resonant and nonresonant strokes of both hands.

Dhaa - TiTaGiRaNaaGa (धा - ति ट गि ड ना ग) - This is a bol expression composed of resonant and nonresonant strokes of both hands.

TiRaKiTaTaKa (ति र कि ट त क) - TiRaKiTaTaKa is a bol expression composed of nonresonant strokes of both hands.

BOLS WHICH HAVE NO TECHNIQUE

There are bols which have no technique. These are simply mnemonics that keep track of the rests and pauses. A (अ), Aa (आ), and I (ई), are the most common. One can also use numbers.

NOTATION

The first set introduced us to our system of notation. Let us review the important points with the following example. This is a mukhada in Kaherava tal.

Example 1 - (Mukhada in Kaherava Tal)

🔊 Listen to Track 1 to hear Example 1

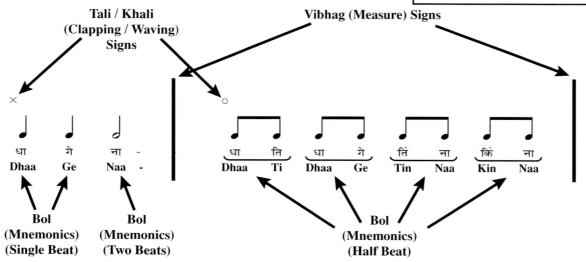

The fact that the strokes on the tabla are represented by syllables is very convenient. All we have to do is to write the syllables down, and we have a basis for musical notation. We have written the syllables in both the middle and lower lines. The middle line contains the traditional notation in Dev Nagri (Hindi/ Sanskrit script). The Roman script transliteration is placed just below this. Try and make a habit of looking only at the middle line. Although it may seem harder at first, it displays subtleties that are lost in transliteration.

The timing is specified two ways; one finds the Western notation in the upper line, while the traditional Indian form is shown in the middle line. In the traditional Indian notation, beats are indicated by tying together the fractions of beats together with a crescent below it. An absence of any tie, means that each syllable is a single beat.

The Western notation is fairly standard and should not require any explanation; however, the rests require some clarification. In this series, we will consider rests as being indistinguishable from elongated notes. For instance, the bottom two examples will be considered synonymous.

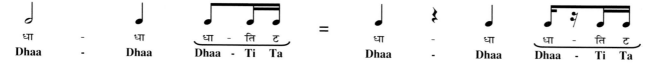

There are also notational elements that are linked to the Indian system of timekeeping. Notice that the vibhags are delineated with several notational elements, the beginning of each vibhag is denoted with a tali/ khali symbol. In example 1, the "X" denotes the first clap; this is also known as the sam. The zero denotes the wave of the hand (khali). The end of each vibhag is denoted by the vertical line. A number is used for all claps other than the sam; for instance "2" denotes the second clap, "3" denotes the third clap, etc.

This is probably all that you need to remember about music notation at this point.

COMPOSITIONAL FORMS

The various bols and their strokes are assembled to create larger rhythmic structures. These structures fall into certain compositional forms. The following forms were introduced in the previous set:

Theka - Theka is the skeletal accompaniment pattern that defines the tal. A number of thekas for the common tals were given in the first book/audio instruction set.

Prakar - Prakar is a variation on the theka. Sometimes these are merely artistic variations. Sometimes, they reflect approaches from the different subtraditions in North Indian music. Sometimes, these variations reflect a technical necessity; for instance, a technique which allows the theka to be played at an unusually high speed. When musicians say that they are playing theka, they are actually playing the various prakars.

A continuous repetition of the pure theka would simply be too boring for anyone to listen to.

Tihai - The tihai is a type of cadence used to bring closure to whatever is being played. It consists of a phrase which is repeated three times such that it ends on sam. Although one occasionally find tihais that are intended to end on beats other than the sam, there are rare.

Kaida - The kaida is a formalized approach to theme-and-variation. It is a structured performance that is usually quite extensive, and is based upon a well defined system of rules. These rules are:

- Overall Structure - One must start with the theka, present an introduction, then proceed with the theme-and-variations, finally bringing things to a close with the tihai.

- Bols - One can only create variations out of the bols of the theme. It is not permissible to suddenly introduce extraneous bols at some point in the variations.

- Progression - The rules of kaida also specify that the variations proceed in a logical, mathematical process. As a general rule, one takes sections of the theme and makes permutations upon them.

- Rhyming Patterns - Another rule of the kaida specifies that the rhyming pattern of each section must be played twice. The first iteration is indicated by the presence of bols with a resonant left hand; Dhaa (धा), Dhin (धिं), and Ga (ग) are common examples. This section is known as the bhari. The second iteration is indicated by bols with an absence of the resonant left hand; Taa (ता), Tin (तिं), and Ka (क) are common examples. This section is known as the khali. (Please note that the use of the term "khali" within this context has nothing to do with the use of the word when describing the wave of the hand for the vibhags.)

- Sub-Theme - There is a sub-theme that is usually present. Dhaa Dhaa Dhin Na (धा धा धिं ना), and Dhin Naa Gin Naa (धिं ना गिं ना) are two well known examples. It is difficult to say whether this last charactristic is a "rule" or merely a common convention.

Whenever one creates theme-and-variations based upon these bols, it is said to be a kaida. This is the benchmark for a formal tabla presentation.

Mukhada - A mukhada is a small flourish culminating on the sam (first beat of the next cycle). Any bol expression may be used as a mukhada.

This completes the review of material covered in the first book/audio set. Let us now move on to concepts that will be necessary in this present work.

OVERVIEW OF DEFINING CRITERIA FOR COMPOSITIONS

It is very easy to get confused as to the definitions of the various compositional forms. Rela, kaida, gat, mukhada, and a score of other terms, tend to be thrown around with great abandon. The situation becomes clear if we look at the different criteria used to define these terms. This is easily illustrated with a simple analogy:

Imagine an alien coming down in a spaceship to study human society. This alien is trying to categorize the various types of people. To accomplish this, he follows an individual without this person's knowledge to see how humans categorize themselves. At one point, the individual under study is referred to as a Democrat; the alien dutifully notes down that this individual is a "Democrat". A little while later, the same individual is described as being a middle-level manager, so the alien scratches off "Democrat", and replaces the entry with "middle-level manager". Some time later the same person is referred to as being a Lutheran. Once again, the alien scratches off "middle level manager" and replaces the entry with "Lutheran". This process continues throughout the day with the same individual being variously described as, a Freemason, a pragmatist, and a host of other terms until finally, the alien gets back in his flying saucer and leaves in utter confusion.

The preceding story is amusing, yet surprisingly similar to the situation of the non-Indian student who is trying to understand the compositional forms. The various terms are bantered about to such a degree that it is difficult for the student to come to grips with their meaning. The situation becomes manageable when we realize that the various forms are defined according to very different criteria. Here is a list of the criteria used to define compositions:

- Structure - Structure is a fairly intuitive concept. This revolves around how a composition is put together. A kaida is very good example of a form which is defined according to its structure.

- Bols - Many times a composition is defined by what kind of bols (syllables) are used. This may not be clear now, but as we look at examples this will become clearer.

- Function - The function is the way that a piece is used. Some forms are only used to open tabla solos, some forms are only used as a type of encore, etc.

- Technique - The technique is sometimes a defining charcteristic. For instance, some forms are defined by the use of only a single hand; some forms are defined by pakhawaj (ancient two-faced drum) technique; some are defined by the usage of both hands on a single drum, etc.

There are two things that should be kept in mind when dealing with criteria. The first is that they are not mutually exclusive, therefore, it is common to find compositions that can be called different things. The second point to keep in mind is that many forms are defined by multiple criteria.

LINGUISTIC DIVERSITY

India is a land of many languages. There are roughly 18 to 20 languages, most of which fall into one of three families of languages. Furthermore, the number of dialects is definitely in the hundreds, and according to some, it well exceeds 1000.

I bring this up because the average user of this series is going to have a teacher under which he or she is studying. Therefore, the chances of all of the terms in this book matching what your teacher gives you, are very small. The important point is that there is no objective benchmark for "correct" terminology. After all, if a mango is called something different every 100 miles, we would certainly expect the musical terms to vary. I submit to you that the musical terms in this series are representative, but it is not to be assumed that these are the only ones.

GHARANA

The gharana system was an important factor in the learning of Indian music. In the past, gharanas functioned in several capacities. As an artistic force, they defined stylistic schools; each gharana developed its own approach to technique and repetoire. Furthermore, the gharanas functioned as a kind of guild; in this capacity they served as a device for allocating royal patronage. Finally, the gharanas were pivotal to the system of education, whereby new musicians were trained to replace older musicians who fell away due to age, infirmity, and death.

The system began to fall away in 20th century; this was due to changing social and cultural conditions. One problem was a fundamental conflict of purpose. The guild aspect of the system required that the number of "qualified" musicians be restricted; this was at odds with the gharana's function to educate new musicians. Furthermore, the artistic inbreeding created musicians that were parochial in their approach to technique and repertoire; "gharanadhar" musicians tended to be restricted in what they could perform. Finally, the demise of the Indian principalities meant that there was no longer any princely patronage that the gharanas could control. Today, the gharanas exist as but a mere shadow of their former glory.

Gharanas may be falling into irrelevance, but they have still left an indelible mark. Their influence may be seen in compositions and techniques in a way that is analogous to the way the Saxons, Goths, Angals, and other vanished peoples, have left their mark on the English language. We will aften allude to elements as being derived from particular gharanas.

LEFT OR RIGHT-HANDEDNESS

This book is written with the presumption that the student is right-handed. This is not to exclude people who are left-handed, but is simply a writing convention to maintain ease in communication. If you are left-handed, simply remember to reverse the hand references throughout this book.

GENDER

The majority of tabla players in India are men. Therefore, we will tend to use masculine forms of the language whenever we are referring to tabla players. This is not to imply that women cannot, or should not play the tabla. This is simply a convention to avoid the editorial nightmare of having to maintain a neutral gender throughout the entire manuscript. This is not to be construed as any prejudice or misogyny, but just an unwillingness to sacrifice clarity of writing for the sake of political correctness. Your indulgence in this matter is humbly requested.

A FEW LAST POINTS

There are a few points to keep in mind concerning the performance of the various examples in this set.

All compositions begin and end with the theka of the appropriate tal. We will try to remind the reader about this point, but do not expect that we will do it every time. By now, you are supposed to know this!

Prakar and theka are synonymous. Whenever the theka is required, a prakar is acceptable. In normal usage, the pure theka is almost never used. Feel free to substitute any prakar that fits the framework and sounds nice. The decision as to how to structure the prakars is primarily based upon artistic considerations; technical considerations are secondary. Many prakars that are technically possible and mathematically functional, just may not sound pleasant when you actually use them. A process of trial and error will help you develop your artistic sense in these matters. Feel free to experiment.

A few words are also in order concerning the speed at which these compositions are played in the audio. I have rendered them at speeds that make the compositions accessible to the typical student. Therefore, they are played considerably slower than one may wish to play them on stage.

SUMMARY

This small introduction is here for several purposes. It reminded us of important material covered in the first volume. It also introduced us to conventions that will be used in this volume. Finally, it presented a few new concepts that are important to our understanding of the subject. Now, let us proceed with our study.

MORE BOLS

This chapter will introduce us to new bols and their techniques. In some cases, these bols are nothing more than different pronunciations. However in other cases, they are totally new, with techniques that we have not previously discussed. We will also discuss the complementary relationship that exists between many bols.

VARIATIONS IN BOLS

There are many reasons why there are variations in the bols. Sometimes these reflect the linguistic diversity in India, for there is a tendency to give the bols an accent according to the language that is found in each geographical region. Sometimes bols are altered to facilitate speed during recitation. Sometimes, the different bols represent different concepts that just happen to share the same technique. For whatever reasons, these inconsistencies create a lot of confusion for the beginning student.

There is a table in the appendix that has a list of many of the common transformations. Please refer to it whenever you feel some doubt about what a particular bol is.

COMPLEMENTARY FORMS

The concept of the complementary forms of the bols is a very important topic. Just as a coin has a different image on each side, or a bookkeeper has to deal with assets as well as liabilities, so too, most of the bols of tabla have two forms.

These forms are easily identified; they are usually identical in every aspect except for the left hand. One class of bols is referred to as "bhari", and has a left-hand technique which shows the presence of resonant strokes. Dhaa (धा), Dhin (धिं), Ga (ग), and Ge (गे) are a few common examples. The other class is known as "khali," and has an absence of resonant strokes of the left hand. Taa (ता), Tin (तिं), Ka (क), Ke (के) are common examples.

Table 1 is a list of complementary bols that we have covered in the first book / audio set of this series ("Learning the Tabla," Mel Bay Publications MB99062M).

For the rest of this series, the new bols will be given in their bhari / khali pairs. This will make the complementary relationship very clear.

Table 1 Khali and Bhari Bols Introduced in First Set	
Khali Form	Bhari Form
Taa (ता) or Naa (ना)	Dhaa (धा)
Tin (तिं) or Tun (तुं)	Dhin (धिं)
Ka (क)	Ga (ग)
Ke (के)	Ge (गे)
Ki Ra Naa Ka (कि ड ना क)	Gi Ra Naa Ga (गि ड ना ग)

It is important to realize that there are exceptions to the system of complementary bols. Some bols simply do not have a complementary form. These are usually the archaic bols from the pakhawaj. These pakhawaj bols will be discussed in a later chapter.

NEW BOLS AND TECHNIQUE

The first volume of this series introduced us to just a few of the bols and bol expressions that are used for tabla. Let us now learn a few more.

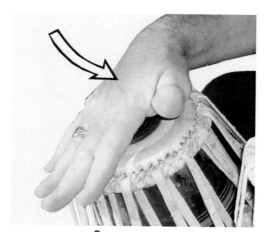

Figure 16. Ti (ति)

Figure 17. Ra (र)

Figure 18. Dhi (धि)

TiRaTiRa (ति र ति र)/**DhiRaDhiRa** (धि र धि र) - These are two of the more interesting techniques of the tabla. Although the tabla is known for its relatively bright and resonant tone, these bols stand out for their dull, muted quality. Their technique is described in table 2.

Here are a few exercises:

Example 2 - Exercise

🔊 Listen to Track 2 to hear Example 2

♩	♩	♩	♩
ति	र	ति	र
Ti	Ra	Ti	Ra

Table 2 TiRaTiRa / DhiRaDhiRa	
TiRaTiRa (ति र ति र) (Khali form)	DhiRaDhiRa (धि र धि र) (Bhari form)
Ti (ति) - This bol is played entirely with the palm of the right hand. For this, one brings the palm of the right hand inward (i.e., toward the body). At the same time, one strikes the dayan with the palm and quickly raises the portion of the palm just under the thumb (see figure 16).	Dhi (धि) - Same as Ti (ति) described in the first column but with a two-finger Ga (see figure 10). Therefore the combination may be seen in figure 18.
Ra (र) -This stroke is made by striking the dayan with the palm of the right hand. However, this is done while the palm is being moved laterally and slightly away from the body (i.e., toward the right). At the time that this is struck, the portion of the palm that is near the little finger is raised slightly (see figure 17).	Ra (र) - Same as the Ra (र) in the first column.
Ti (ति) - Same as the last Ti (see figure 16)	Dhi (धि) - Same as the Ti (ति) in the first column. Please note that in spite of the bol, there is no resonant left hand. The presumption is that the sound of the Ga will still be resonating from the first Dhi (धि)
Ra (र) - Same as last Ra (see figure 17)	Ra (र) - Same as the Ra (र) in the first column.

Example 3 - Exercise

🔊 Listen to Track 3 to hear Example 3

♩ ♩ ♩ ♩
धि | र | धि | र
Dhi | **Ra** | **Dhi** | **Ra**

TiRaTiRaKiRaNaaKa (ति र ति र कि ड ना क) / **DhiRaDhiRaGiRaNaaGa** (धि र धि र गि ड ना ग) - These are nothing more than the previous TiRaTiRa (ति र ति र)/ DhiRaDhiRa (धि र धि र) with the addition of the phrase KiRaNaaKa (कि ड ना क) or GiRaNaaGa (गि ड ना ग). Their techniques are described in the table 3.

Here are some exercises for this bol:

Example 4 - Exercise

🔊 Listen to Track 4 to hear Example 4

♩ ♩ ♩ ♩ ♩ ♩ ♩ ♩
ति | र | ति | र | कि | ड | ना | क
Ti | **Ra** | **Ti** | **Ra** | **Ki** | **Ra** | **Naa** | **Ka**

Table 3	
TiRaTiTaKiRaNaaKa / DhiRaDhiRaGiRaNaaGa	
TiRaTiRaKiDaNaaKa (ति र ति र कि ड ना क) (Khali Form)	DhiRaDhiRaGiDaNaaGa (धि र धि र गि ड ना ग) (Bhari Form)
TiRaTiRa (ति र ति र) - TiRaTiRa is played exactly as it was in Table 2.	DhiRaDhiRa (धि र धि र) - DhiRaDhiRa is played exactly as it was in Table 2.
Ki (कि) - Flat, nonresonant slap of the left hand (see figure 12)	Gi (गि) - two-finger Ga (ग) (figure 10
Ra (ड) - Bring the last two fingers of the right hand down against the edge of the dayan with a dull nonresonant sound (see figure 4).	Ra (ड) - Same as first column (figure 4)
Naa (ना) - Standard rim stroke of the right hand (see figure 2)	Naa (ना) - Same as first column (figure 2)
Ka (क) - Flat, nonresonant slap of the left hand (see figure 12)	Ga (ग) - one finger Ga (ग) (figure 11)

Example 5 - Exercise

🔊 Listen to Track 5 to hear Example 5

♩ ♩ ♩ ♩ ♩ ♩ ♩ ♩
धि | र | धि | र | गि | ड | ना | ग
Dhi | **Ra** | **Dhi** | **Ra** | **Gi** | **Ra** | **Naa** | **Ga**

16

Taa - Taa - TiRaKiTaTaKaTaa - TiRaKiTa (ता - ता - तिरकिटतकता - तिरकिट) / **Dhaa - Dhaa - TiRaKiTaTaKaTaa - TiRaKiTa** (धा - धा - तिरकिटतकता - तिरकिट) -This is a very beautiful and useful bol expression. There are numerous ways to execute it, but one of the most efficient techniques involves a curious interplay of both Delhi and Purbi techniques. This approach is shown in table 4.

Table 4	
Taa - Taa - TiRaKiTaTaKaTaa - TiRaKiTa / Dhaa - Dhaa - TiRaKiTaTaKaTaa - TiRaKiTa	
Taa - Taa - TiRaKiTaTaKaTaa - TiRaKiTa (ता - ता - तिरकिटतकता - तिरकिट) (Khali Form)	Dhaa - Dhaa - TiRaKiTaTaKaTaa - TiRaKiTa (धा - धा - तिरकिटतकता - तिरकिट) (Bhari Form)
Taa (ता) Delhi style (index finger on chat) (figure 2)	Dhaa (धा) Same as first column but with two-finger Ga (ग) (figure 14)
Taa (ता) Delhi style (index finger on chat) (figure 2)	Dhaa (धा) Same as first column but with two - finger Ga (ग) (figure 14)
Ti (ति) Delhi style (middle finger on syahi) (figure 6)	Ti (ति) Same as first column (figure 6)
Ra (र) Index finger on syahi (figure 8)	Ra (र) Same as first column (figure 8)
Ki (कि) Standard left hand Ka (क) (figure 12)	Ki (कि) Same as first column (figure 12)
Ta (ट) Last three fingers of right hand (purbi style) (figure 9)	Ta (ट) Same as first column (figure 9)
Ta (त) Index finger on syahi (figure 8)	Ta (त) Same as first column (figure 8)
Ka (क) Standard left hand Ka (क) (figure 12)	Ka (क) Same as first column (figure 12)
Taa (ता) Delhi style (index finger on chat) (figure 2)	Taa (ता) Same as first column (figure 2)
Ti (ति) Delhi style (middle finger on syahi) (figure 6)	Ti (ति) Same as first column (figure 6)
Ra (र) Index finger on syahi (figure 8)	Ra (र) Same as first column (figure 8)
Ki (कि) Standard left hand Ka (क) (figure 12)	Ki (कि) Same as first column (figure 12)
Ta (ट) Last two fingers of right hand (nonresonant) (figure 4)	Ta (ट) Same as first column (see figure 4)

Example 6 - Exercise

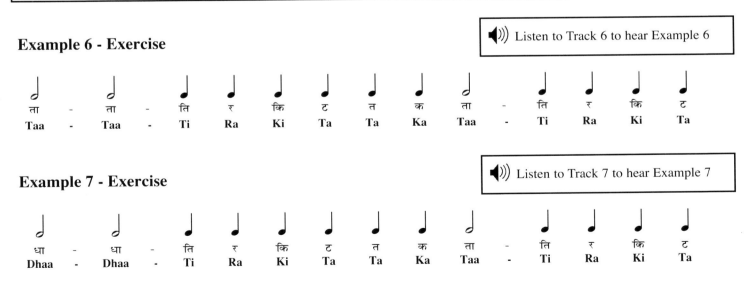

| 🔊))) Listen to Track 6 to hear Example 6 |

ता - ता - तिर किट तक ता - तिर किट
Taa - Taa - Ti Ra Ki Ta Ta Ka Taa - Ti Ra Ki Ta

Example 7 - Exercise

| 🔊))) Listen to Track 7 to hear Example 7 |

धा - धा - तिर किट तक ता - तिर किट
Dhaa - Dhaa - Ti Ra Ki Ta Ta Ka Taa - Ti Ra Ki Ta

SUMMARY

This chapter acquainted us with a number of new concepts and forms. We learned the concept of the complementary bol; complementary bols are those which are considered to be conceptually equivalent except for the presence or absence of the resonant left hand. A number of complementary bols were introduced in the first volume, but they were not explicitly presented as such. We learned several new ones in this chapter.

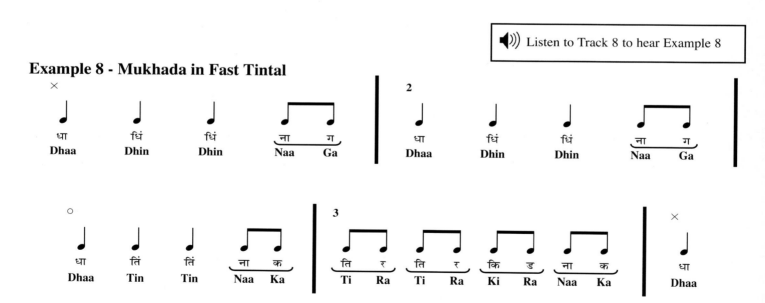

MUKHADA & TUKADA

This chapter introduces us to many new mukhadas as well as the concept of the tukada. The tukada is a form that is very similar to the mukhada. Often the two overlap, whereby the same composition may be considered to be either one. This chapter will also allow us to take some of the exercises that we learned in the last chapter and use them in the form of mukhadas and tukadas.

Both mukhadas and tukadas are small cadential forms which culminate on the first beat of the cycle (i.e., the sam). Functionally, they are about the same. In almost any situation where you use a mukhada, a tukada will work just as well. The major difference is in their overall length. This will be explained in greater detail.

MUKHADA

The mukhada was briefly introduced in the first volume of this series. However, it is appropriate for us to look into it more thoroughly.

The term "mukhada" literally means a "mouth" or a "face". This enigmatic name begins to make sense when we look at a secondary meaning of the word. In a very common classical vocal form known as "kheyal", there is a small rhythmic passage which culminates on the sam; this is known as the mukhada. Interestingly enough, the tabla mukhada is also a small flourish which culminates on the sam. This appears to be the origin of the term.

The structure of the mukhada is not highly developed. A mukhada is seldom more than one cycle, usually it is only the last few beats; therefore, it is not long enough to develop any real structure.

Mukhada in Tintal - Here is a mukhada that is based upon a bol that was introduced in the last chapter. One may wish to refer back to table 3 for a discussion of its technique.

> 🔊 Listen to Track 8 to hear Example 8

Example 8 - Mukhada in Fast Tintal

Please note that any prakar is acceptable. The one in this example is slightly different from our "official" theka. Notice that the last beat of the first, second, and third vibhags are a NaaGa (ना ग) /NaaKa(ना क) instead of the more usual Dhaa (धा). We are noting this one, but throughout the rest of this series we will not bother to specify any particular prakar. **The text may note a simple theka, but the recorded example may use a different prakar.** This will reinforce the idea that the various prakars are interchangeable and do not have any real theoretical importance.

It is also important to note where the theka / prakar ends and the mukhada begins. In this example, it is only the last four beats and the sam that are the mukhada. Please notice that the sam is included. The entire purpose of the mukhada is to stress this first beat. Since the sam is included, we could argue that this mukhada is actually five beats and not four.

Example 9 - Mukhada in Tintal - (Please note that any Tintal prakar is acceptable). Please refer back to table 3 for a discussion of the technique.

Example 10 - Mukhada in Tintal - Please refer back to table 4 for a discussion of the technique.

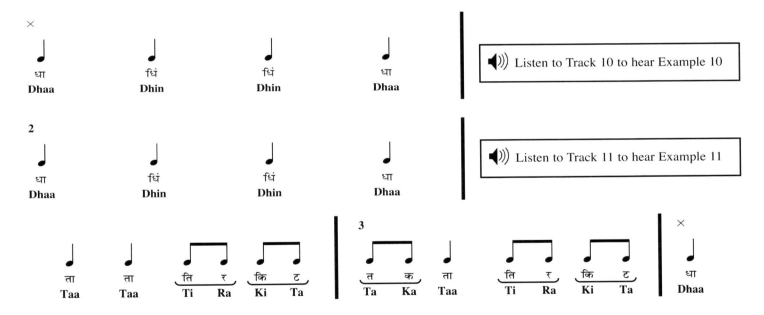

Example 11 - Mukhada in Tintal - Please refer back to table 4 for a discussion of the technique

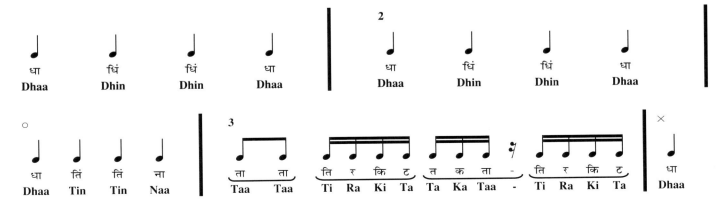

19

Example 12 - Mukhada in Jhaptal - The technique for the mukhada is shown in table 4.

Listen to Track 12 to hear Example 12

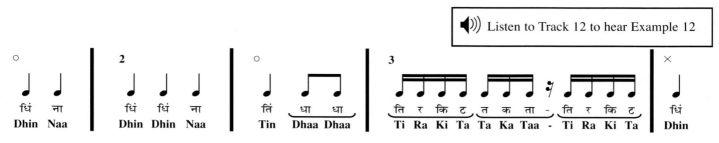

TUKADA

The term "tukada" literally means a "piece." It is a small composition that is used to emphasize the sam (first beat). Functionally, it is very similar to mukhada; yet structurally, it is different. Where the mukhada is too short to develop any real structure, the tukada is much larger; therefore, some type of rudimentary structure is possible.

The structure of the tukada is simple. It is usually a small body of bols followed by an ending; this is usually a very small tihai. The tukada is often one to two cycles in length. Here are a few tukadas based upon familiar bols:

Example 13 - Tukada in Tintal

Listen to Track 13 to hear Example 13

Body of Tukada

Ending

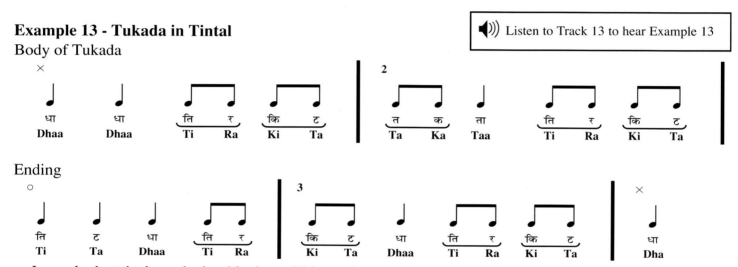

Let us look at the last tukada a bit closer. This one is very short; it is so short that it impinges upon our mukhada. If this were to be played in double time, it would only take half a cycle, in which case it would be more correct to call it a mukhada. The ending of this tukada is interesting. It has a basic quality of a tihai, but upon close examination we find the structure is just not quite long enough or well defined to be called a tihai. Such cadential forms are common in the lighter styles of music.

Example 14 - Tukada in Tintal - Here is an example which is of the length and structure that is typical of the tukada. It has a short body followed by a tihai.

Listen to Track 14 to hear Example 14

Body of Tukada

Tihai

Tukada in Tintal - Here is an example of a tukada which is rather long. Notice that the body is so long that it has started to develop an internal structure of its own. One could argue that the body has become a rela. (The rela is discussed in chapter 5.)

Example 15 - Tukada in Tintal
Body of Tukada

Tihai

Listen to Track 16 to hear Example 16

Example 16

SUMMARY

This section covered various material. It discussed the mukhada and tukada. It also gave us an opportunity to take some of the new bols that we learned in the previous chapter and put them together in ways that are practical.

Our discussion of the mukhada and the tukada clarified a number of points. We have seen that the mukhada and tukada are similar in that they are both short cadential forms that emphasise the sam (first beat of the cycle). However, "short" is a relative term. The mukhada is so short that virtually no structure is possible. In contrast, the tukada is long enough to develop a rudimentary two part structure; there is a simple body, followed by some type of cadence; this is usually a small tihai.

NEW TECHNIQUES FOR FAMILIAR BOLS

This chapter will return us to some very familiar bols. However, we will look at some new techniques for them.

The concept of having multiple techniques for common bols is similar to having a tool box with multiple sizes of screwdrivers, allen wrenches, etc. Imagine yourself having only one screwdriver; you are in trouble. There will be times that it is the wrong type, the wrong length, or the wrong size. Having the wrong screwdriver is as bad as having no screwdriver at all. This is analogous to the situation with the bols. There is no single technique which is universally applicable. Although a particular technique may serve well within one situation, it may fail in another.

This brings up the very natural question as to what factors determine which technique to use. In general, the factors are:

* Implied Style - Sometimes, a style is implied by the composition. Just as urban English is implied for rap music or Elizabethan English is implied for Shakespearean plays, in a similar way, particular techniques are implied for certain tabla compositions. This requires a greater knowledge of compositional theory than we have now, so we must discuss this in a later volume.

* Speed - The speed of the performance is a very important factor in determining which techniques should be used. As a general rule, there are techniques which are rich in texture, yet poor in their ability to be played fast. This is in contrast to other techniques which are efficient and allow for high speed, but may be deficient in texture and variety of sound. One should be familiar with the various techniques and be able to use different ones according to the situation.

* Transitions - Bol expressions are frequently linked together to form larger compositions. This creates a very strong incentive to alter the technique of the bol at the place where transitions occur. This creates a situation where the leading stroke and the last stroke of any bol expression are determined in part by adjacent techniques. Therefore, the initial and final bols may be considered to be inherently ambiguous. This is a very important consideration, one that we will devote an entire chapter to later in this book.

* Personal Preference - One generally has a great degree of flexibility as to what techniques can be used. One will seldom have a particular style implied, and in most situations there will not be any overriding technical reason to use one particular technique over another. Therefore, personal preference is the only reason why one will chose a particular technique.

We have discussed some of the reasons for there being different techniques. Let us now look at particular examples of alternate techniques for bols that we are already familiar with.

DHIN

We became familiar with Dhin (धिं) in the first volume (figure 13). For this, we strike with the index finger in a resonant fashion, at the place where the syahi and the maidan come together; at the same time we play Ga (ग) with the left hand.

There is an alternate form which is very beautiful. For this, we simply mix Ga (ग) (figure 10) with Toon (तूं) (figure 7). This is illustrated in the following exercise:

Example 17 - Exercise

धिं   धिं   धिं   धिं

Dhin   **Dhin**   **Dhin**   **Dhin**

Listen to Track 17 to hear Example 17

TITA

TiTa (ति ट) is one of the most fundamental bols of the tabla. In the last volume we dealt with only two types, a Delhi style and a Purbi style. We will begin our discussion here with five types. We will refer to these types as a standard Delhi style, a reverse Delhi style, a standard Purbi style, a reverse Purbi style, and a folk style.

It is helpful to have a series of tests that we can apply to the various techniques. These allow us to gauge the advantages and disadvantages of each approach. The following exercises make good tests:

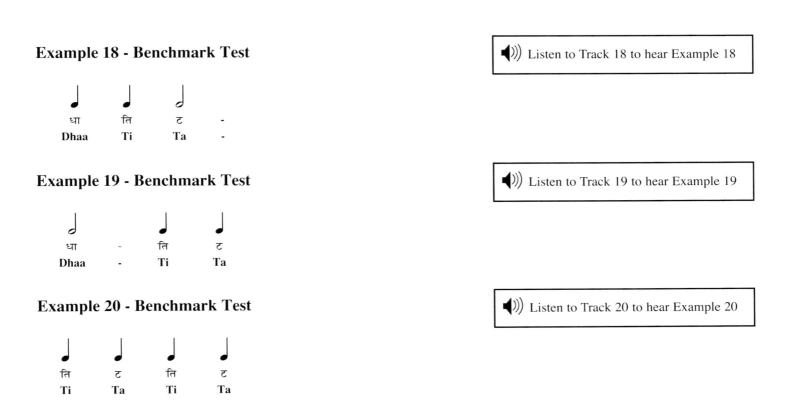

Example 18 - Benchmark Test

Listen to Track 18 to hear Example 18

धा   ति   ट   -

Dhaa   **Ti**   **Ta**   -

Example 19 - Benchmark Test

Listen to Track 19 to hear Example 19

धा   -   ति   ट

Dhaa   -   **Ti**   **Ta**

Example 20 - Benchmark Test

Listen to Track 20 to hear Example 20

ति   ट   ति   ट

Ti   **Ta**   **Ti**   **Ta**

Standard Delhi - This style is often considered to be the "pure" tabla technique. This is not to be construed as a statement of any superiority; it merely means that this technique is not derived from pakhawaj or any other Indian drum. This technique is executed as shown in table 5.

Here is how the standard Delhi TiTa (ति ट) stands up in these exercises. The exercise in example 18 shows the strength of this style. It is safe to say that no other technique has the efficiency in movement that this technique shows within this context. The exercise in example 19 on the other hand shows a weakness of the Delhi TiTa (ति ट). Although it is functional in slow to moderately fast speeds, its inefficiency hampers efforts to play at very high speeds.

The applicability of the Delhi TiTa (ति ट) for exercise in example 20 shows somewhat mixed results. Speed is no problem, but the Delhi TiTa (ति ट) is rather soft in its tone. If your artistic vision calls for delicacy, then it is effective. However, if one is looking for a sense of depth and power, then this technique fails miserably. I think that most musicians would agree that it is rather weak in these situations.

Reverse Delhi - We can reverse the strokes in our Delhi TiTa (ति ट) for an interesting effect. We play this form by using the technique shown in table 6. We now find that the exercise in example 18 is awkward to play in extremely high speeds, while the exercise shown in example 19 is efficient. The exercise in example 20 is about the same as it was with the standard Delhi style.

Standard Purbi - The standard Purbi TiTa (ति ट) was introduced in the first instruction book/cd set. Its technique is shown in table 7.

When we apply a standard Purbi technique to the previous exercises, we see some interesting things. We find that when it is applied to the exercise in example 18 or the exercise in example 19, it is not particularly efficient. It does not matter how much one practices, one will never reach the potential speed of an appropriately selected Delhi technique. However, the exercise in example 20 shows the real strength of this approach. No Delhi technique will come anywhere near the power, speed, and majesty that the Purbi technique displays within this context.

Reverse Purbi - The reverse Purbi TiTa (ति ट) is executed by the technique shown in table 8; let us look at the relative advantages and disadvantages. We see that the reverse TiTa (ति ट) is not particularly efficient in the exercise in example 18. However, it truly shines in the exercise in example 20, where it is very efficient and much more powerful than any Delhi technique. In the exercise shown in example 19, it is much more efficient than a standard Purbi version, but not the most efficient one possible. Still, it is clearly more powerful than either of our Delhi techniques.

Folk TiTa - This is a very unusual TiTa (ति ट). Its technique is shown in table 9. The key to this technique's efficiency is that when the last two fingers are brought down, they will be brought down directly to our "home position" (i.e. the finger position from which Naa (ना), Tin (तिं), and many other strokes are played).

The application of this technique is very interesting. It is acceptable for the exercises in examples 18 and 20, but not exceptional; one would probably wish to use other forms of TiTa (ति ट) when faced with these situations. However, the exercise in example 19 shows the advantage of this technique. No other technique has the potential speed or efficiency when faced with this type of movement.

It would appear that having a technique that is only applicable for one context would severely limit its utility. However, this is one of the most common movements in tabla; therefore, this technique turns out to be one of the most useful. If you master this approach, it will allow you to play many potentially awkward bols with great speed and ease.

Table 5 Standard Delhi TiTa
Ti (ति) - Middle finger of right hand (figure 6)
Ta (ट) - Index finger of right hand (figure 8)

Table 6 Reverse Delhi TiTa
Ti (ति) - Index finger of right hand (figure 8)
Ta (ट) - Middle finger of right hand (figure 6)

Table 7 Standard Purbi TiTa
Ti (ति) - Last three finger of right hand (figure 9)
Ta (ट) - Index fingers of right hand (figure 8)

Table 8 Reverse Purbi TiTa
Ti (ति) - index finger of right hand (figure 8)
Ta (ट) - Last three fingers of right hand (figure 9)

Table 9 Folk TiTa
Ti (ति) - Index finger of right hand (figure 8)
Ta (ट) - Last three fingers of right hand (figure 4)

TIRAKITA

We have various types of TiRaKiTa (तिरकिट) just as we have various types of TiTa (तिट). One time I set out to count the number of TiRaKiTa's (तिरकिट) that I had encountered. I passed 20 when I just got tired of counting them. In this section we will look at four types. We will refer to these as the Delhi style, Purbi style, and two mixed versions.

Delhi TiRaKiTa - The Delhi TiRaKiTa (तिरकिट) is executed by the technique shown in Table 10. It is interesting to note that the term "Delhi" (a.k.a. Dilli) is really a misnomer. It is actually a technique that was developed in Ajrada. Originally, the final Ta (ट) was played with the middle finger; however, the Delhi tabla players abandoned this technique a long time ago. Today, this Ajrada innovation has come to be referred to as the Delhi form.

Table 10 Delhi TiRaKiTa (a.k.a. Modern Dilli or Ajrad Style)
Ti (ति) - Middle finger of right hand (figure 6)
Ra (र) - Index finger of right hand (figure 8)
Ki (कि) - Left hand nonresonant (i.e., Ka)
Ta (ट) - Last two fingers of right hand (figure 4)

The relative strengths and weaknesses of this technique are easily illustrated. The exercise in example 21 shows the greatest strength of the Delhi TiRaKiTa. No other style has the same efficiency when faced with this situation.

Example 21 - Exercise

ति	र	कि	ट
Ti	**Ra**	**Ki**	**Ta**

> 🔊 Listen to Track 21 to hear Example 21

We must remember that speed and efficiency are not always going to be our top priority. If we are looking for power, we find that the standard Delhi technique is simply too weak.

Purbi TiRaKiTa - The Purbi TiRaKiTa (तिरकिट) is executed by the technique shown in table 11.

There are advantages and disadvantages to this technique. Its strong point is its feeling of power; if this is your artistic requirement, then nothing else will do the job. Unfortunately, this technique is often awkward and will fail to give you speed in the majority of contexts. This weakness is clearly shown when we attempt to play the exercise in example 21. The continuous repetition of the movement of the last three fingers (figure 9) is an obstacle which will constantly limit our speed.

Table 11 Purbi TiRaKiTa (a.k.a. Pakhawaj Style)
Ti (ति) - Last three fingers of right hand (figure 9)
Ra (र) - Index finger of right hand (figure 8)
Ki (कि) - Left hand nonresonant (i.e., Ka) (figure 12)
Ta (ट) - Last three fingers of right hand (figure 9)

Mixed TiRaKiTa #1 - TiRaKiTa (तिरकिट) is a very good candidate for mixing Delhi and Purbi approaches. When properly handled, a combination can produce a technique which has a balance of speed and power. A typical technique is shown in table 12. Here is an exercise, that shows the strength of this technique:

Example 22 - Exercise

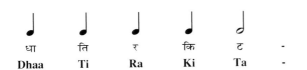

धा	ति	र	कि	ट	-
Dhaa	**Ti**	**Ra**	**Ki**	**Ta**	-

> 🔊 Listen to Track 22 to hear Example 22

Table 12 Mixed TiRaKiTa #1
Ti (ति) - Middle finger of right hand (figure 6)
Ra (र) - Index finger of right hand (figure 8)
Ki (कि) - Left hand in a nonresonant fashion (i.e., Ka) (figure 12)
Ta (ट) - Last three fingers of right hand (figure 9)

The context that we have just described is not common. In ordinary usage, we find that starting a TiRaKiTa (ति र कि ट) with either a Delhi or Purbi approach is not going to make that much of a difference. However, the next example is a mixed form that is extremely useful:

Mixed TiRaKiTa #2 - This is perhaps one of the most useful forms of TiRaKiTa (ति र कि ट). Its technique is shown in table 13. The strength of this technique is that the last stroke returns us to our home position. Therefore, no repositioning of the hands is required to execute the next stroke.

Here is an exercise to show the strength of the mixed TiRaKiTa in table 13:

Example 23 - Exercise

🔊)) Listen to Track 23 to hear Example 23

धा	-	ति	र	कि	ट
Dhaa	-	Ti	Ra	Ki	Ta

TAA - TITAKIRANAAKA & DHAA - TITAGIRANAAGA
This is an alternate form of Dhaa - TiTaGiRaNaaGa that was introduced in the first volume. Let us look at a form which takes a more Purbi approach. Its technique is shown in table 14.

Table 13 Mixed TiRaKiTa #2
Ti (ति) - Last three fingers of right hand (figure 9)
Ra (र) - Index finger of right hand (figure 8)
Ki (कि) - Left hand nonresonant fashion (i.e., Ka) (figure 12)
Ta (ट) - Last two fingers of right hand (figure 4)

26

Here are two exercises to help us become familiar with this technique.

Example 24 - Exercise

🔊)) Listen to Track 24 to hear Example 24

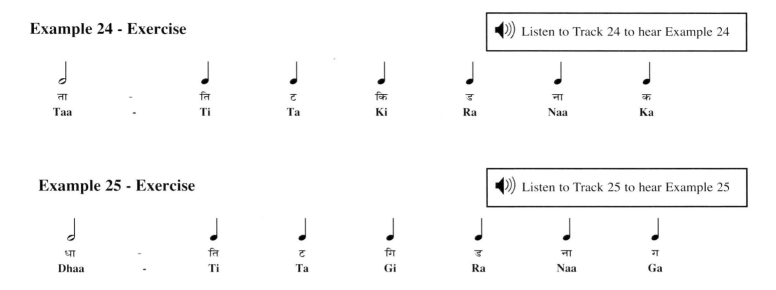

| Taa | - | Ti | Ta | Ki | Ra | Naa | Ka |

Example 25 - Exercise

🔊)) Listen to Track 25 to hear Example 25

| Dhaa | - | Ti | Ta | Gi | Ra | Naa | Ga |

One cannot help but notice that in the last two exercises that the normal Naa (ना) has been replaced by a non-resonant stroke. This is sometimes done to gain speed.

Table 14 Taa - TiTaKiRaNaaKa / Dhaa - TiTaGiRaNaaGa	
Taa - Ti Ta Ki Ra Naa Ka (ता - ति ट कि ड ना क)	Dhaa - Ti Ta Gi Ra Naa Ga (धा - ति ट गि ड ना ग)
Taa (ता) One finger on chaat as shown in figure 2	Dhaa (धा) Same as first column but with two-finger Ga (figure 14)
Ti (ति) - Three fingers of right hand (figure 9)	Ti (ति) - Three fingers of right hand (figure 9)
Ta (ट) - Index finger of right hand (figure 8)	Ta (ट) - Index finger of right hand (figure 8)
Ki (कि) - Left hand nonresonant (i.e., Ka) (figure 12)	Gi (गि) - Two-finger Ga (figure 10)
Ra (ड) - Last three fingers of right hand (figure 9)	Ra (ड) - Same as left hand column (figure 9)
Naa (ना) - Index finger of right hand (nonresonant) (Figure 8)	Naa (ना) - Same as left hand column (figure 8)
Ka (क) - Left hand nonresonant (i.e., Ka) (figure 12)	Ga (ग) - Index finger Ga (figure 11)

TIRATIRAKIRANAAKA & DHIRADHIRAGIRANAAGA
This is an alternate form of DhiRaDhiRaGiDaNaaGa that was introduced in the chapter entitled "More Bols". The TiRaTiRa (DhiRaDhiRa) section may be kept the same, but we can use the abbreviated form of GiRaNaaGa in a manner similar to what we used in the preceding discussion. This is shown in table 15. Here are two exercises:

Example 26 - Exercise

🔊))) Listen to Track 26 to hear Example 26

♩	♩	♩	♩	♩	♩	♩	♩
ति	र	ति	त	कि	ड	ना	क
Ti	Ra	Ti	Ra	Ki	Ra	Naa	Ka

Example 27 - Exercise

🔊))) Listen to Track 27 to hear Example 27

♩	♩	♩	♩	♩	♩	♩	♩
धि	र	धि	र	गि	ड	ना	ग
Dhi	Ra	Dhi	Ra	Gi	Ra	Naa	Ga

Table 15 TiRaTiRaKiRaNaaKa / DhiRaDhiRaGiRaNaaGa	
TiRaTiRaKiRaNaaKa (ति र ति कि ट ना क) Khali Form	DhiRaDhiRaGiRaNaaGa (धि र धि र गि ड ना ग) Bhari Form
Ti (ति) - This bol is played entirely with the palm of the right hand. For this, one brings the palm of the right hand inward (i.e., toward the left hand). At the same time, one strikes the drum with the palm and quickly raises the portion of the palm near the thumb (figure 16)	Dhi (धि) - Same as first column but with a two-finger bayan (figure 10)
Ra (र) - Ra is made by striking the dayan with the palm of the right hand. However, this is done while the palm is being moved laterally away from the body (i.e. toward the right). At the time that this is struck, the portion of the palm near the little finger is raised slightly (figure 17).	Ra (र) - Same as first column.
Ti (ति) - Same as the last Ti (figure 16).	Dhi (धि) - Same as first column. Please note that in spite of the bol, there is no resonant left hand.
Ra (र) - Same as last Ra (figure 17).	Ra (र) - Same as first column. (figure 17)
Ki (कि) - Left hand nonresonant (i.e., Ka) (figure 12).	Gi (गि) - two-finger Ga (figure 10).
Ra (ड) - This is an alternate technique. It is the last three fingers of right hand (figure 9).	Ra (ड) - Same as left hand column (figure 9)
Naa (ना) - This is an alternate technique. It is the index finger of right hand (nonresonant) (figure 8)	Naa (ना) - Same as left hand column (figure 8)
Ka (क) - Left hand nonresonant (i.e., Ka) (figure 12).	Ga (ग) - Index finger Ga (figure 11).

FAST PAKARS

It is often necessary to play thekas at a very high speeds. Sometimes these speeds necessitate unusual prakars and techniques in order to be able to keep up the tempo. Here are a few very useful ones.

Fast Tintal Prakar - Here is a version of Tintal that is very appropriate for faster styles of playing. With this technique, one can play at moderately high speeds for a long time without getting tired. This may be used in a variety of settings including kathak dance, instrumental, and vocal music. The bols are:

Example 28
Fast Tintal prakar

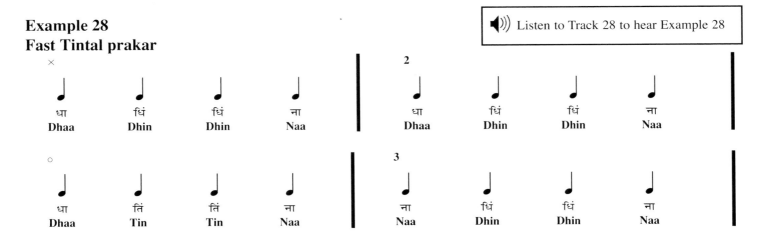

🔊))) Listen to Track 28 to hear Example 28

×			
धा	धिं	धिं	ना
Dhaa	Dhin	Dhin	Naa

The bols do not indicate anything unusual. Indeed these bols are commonly played for Tintal in the medium speeds. However, the technique behind this prakar is stunning, and is what really makes this work. The technique is described in table 16.

Let us make a few observations about this technique. Notice that for each vibhag, the right hand technique remains unchanged. Essentially, the right hand is just cranking out an endless "Naa Ti Ta Naa". However, the left hand varies to maintain the khali/tali structure. This prakar simply does not work in slow, medium or even modestly fast tempos. It really must be played at high speed in order to fully express its Tintal character.

Fast Dadra Prakar - This is a prakar of Dadra which is easy to execute at high speeds. This version may be used for film songs, qawwali, and similar light music. Here is the bol:

Example 29 - Fast Dadra Prakar

Table 16
Fast Tintal
Dhaa (धा) - Standard Dhaa with two-finger bayan (figure 14)
Dhin (धिं) - Middle finger in nonresonant fashion (figure 6) (i.e, Tee) along with index-finger bayan (figure 11)
Dhin (धिं) - Index finger in nonresonant fashion (figure 8) along with two-finger bayan (figure 10)
Naa (ना) - Standard Naa (figure 2)
Dhaa (धा) - Standard Dhaa with 2 finger bayan (figure 14)
Dhin (धिं) - Middle finger in nonresonant fashion (figure 6)(i.e, Tee) along with one-finger bayan (figure 11)
Dhin (धिं) - Index finger in nonresonant fashion (figure 8) along with two-finger bayan (figure 10)
Naa (ना) - Standard Naa (figure 2)
Dhaa (धा) - Standard Dhaa with two-finger bayan (figure 14)
Tin (तिं) - Middle finger in nonresonant fashion (i.e., Tee) (figure 6)
Tin (तिं) - Index finger in nonresonant fashion (figure 8)
Naa (ना) - Standard Naa (figure 2)
Naa (ना) - Standard Naa (figure 2)
Dhin (धिं) - Middle finger in nonresonant fashion (figure 6)(i.e, Tee) along with one-finger bayan (figure 11)
Dhin (धिं) - Index finger in nonresonant fashion (figure 8) along with two-finger bayan (figure 10)
Naa (ना) - Standard Naa (figure 2)

 🔊))) Listen to Track 29 to hear Example 29

Table 17 **Fast Dadra Tal**
Dhin (धिं) - Middle finger in nonresonant fashion on dayan (figure 6) with two-finger Ga (figure 10)
Tin (तिं) - Index finger in nonresonant fashion on dayan (figure 8)
Naa (ना) - Standard Naa (figure 2)
Dhin (धिं) - Middle finger in nonresonant fashion on dayan (figure 6) with index finger bayan Ga (figure 11)
Dhin (धिं) - Index finger in nonresonant fashion on dayan (figure 8) with two-finger Ga (figure 10)
Naa (ना) - Standard Naa (figure 2)

Let us look at this technique in greater detail. We see that the right hand repeats a simple "Ti Ta Naa" pattern for each vibhag, while the bayan cuts across the vibhags in an interesting way. The left hand should emphasize the first and the fifth beat, while the right hand should emphasize the third and the sixth beat. The result is a very interesting bounce that makes this prakar very appealing.

SUMMARY

We have seen that it is very important to have multiple techniques for our material. The reasons for the various techniques are varied; but the bottom line is simple. No single technique is universally applicable. One will constantly come upon situations were there is a stylistic, artistic, or a technical reason to use a particular technique at the exclusion of others. This should not be seen as complicating the situation. Instead, we should look at this as a reflection of the richness of the field of tabla.

RELA

The rela is a very common form of composition. The most distinctive quality is its high speed. This causes the rela to be defined both by its function and as well as by its bol. Functionally, it is useful in solos and in accompaniment situations where tabla players are allowed to "strut their stuff". As such, it is a heavy display of the tabla player's skill. Bols also play a part in defining the rela, because only those bols that can be played at high speeds are used.

I should like to make one point clear about the examples on this audio recording. These examples are played considerably slower than I would recommend for stage purposes. They have been slowed down to make them clear and accessible to the beginning tabla student.

BEGINNER'S PRACTICE RELA #1

Here is a little rela that is good for the beginner. The bols are fairly easy yet it has a very nice feel when played at a brisk speed. There are only two bol expressions in this rela. There is DhiRaDhiRaGiRaNaaGa (see table 3) and its khali form, TiRaTiRaKiRaNaaKa (also in table 3). This rela is shown below:

> 🔊)) Listen to Track 30 to hear Example 30

Example 30 - Practice Rela in Tintal

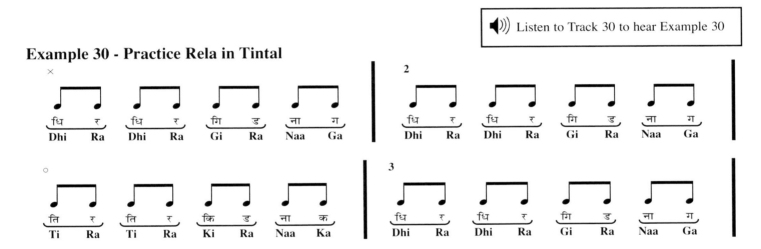

BEGINNER'S PRACTICE RELA #2

This too, is a nice rela for the beginner. It is good practice for the types of bols that one will use for the rest of ones performing career. Start slowly, but try and bring it to a very brisk speed. It is based upon the bols Dhaa - TiTaGiRaNaaGa, and its khali form, Taa - TiTaKiraNaaKa. These were both discussed at great length in the first book/CD set.

> 🔊)) Listen to Track 31 to hear Example 31

Example 31 - Practice Rela in Tintal

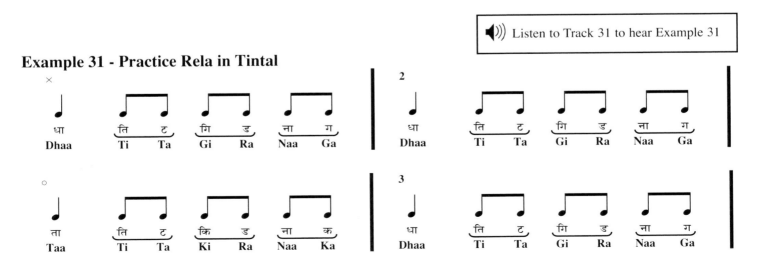

STRUCTURE OF RELA

Structure is conspicuously absent in defining the rela. However, it is normal for musicians to try and place the rela within some type of structural context. Therefore, it is common to view relas as existing upon a continuum. This continuum has at one extreme a highly structured form known as "kaida rela". It has at the opposite end a highly improvised and unstructured form which is known as "swatantra rela". Relas may exist at any point between these two extremes.

Swatantra Rela
(freeform)

Kaida Rela
(structured)

Figure 19. Rela Continuum

KAIDA-RELA

The kaida-rela is the most structured form of a rela. It is easy to visualize this as consisting of bols that are executed at a very high speed, but strictly adhering to the form and development of the kaida.

Kaida-Rela in Tintal - The following is a good example of a kaida-rela. This clearly shows the form and structure of the kaida. There are several interesting bols for this composition. Dhaa - TiTaGiRaNaaGa and its khali form Taa - TiTaKiRaNaaKa were discussed in the first volume of this set. DhiRaDhiRaGiRaNaaGa and its khali form TiRaTiRaKiRaNaaKa were discussed in table 15. If there are any questions as to their technique, one should review the appropriate sections.

🔊)) Listen to Track 32 to hear Example 32

Example 32 - Kaida/Rela in Tintal

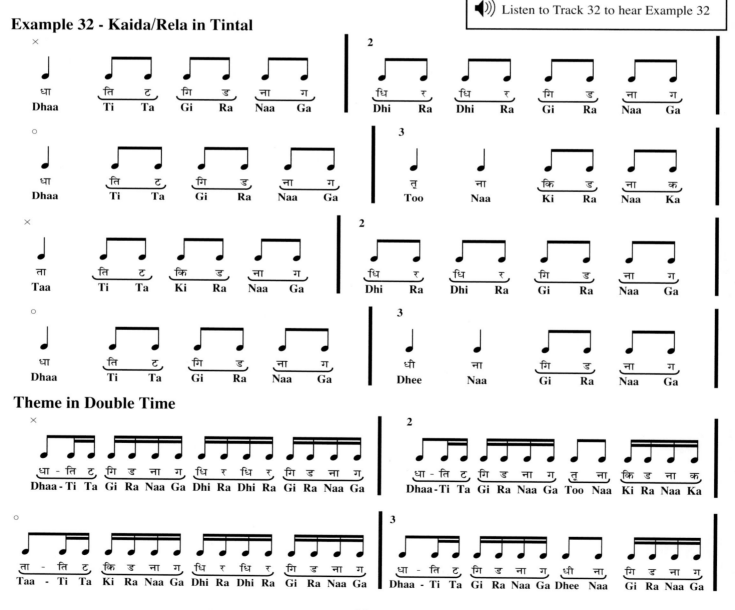

Theme in Double Time

Repetition of Theme in Double Time

Variation #1

Variation #2

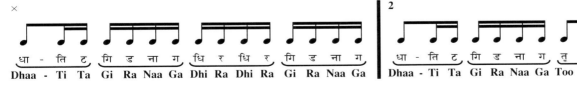

33

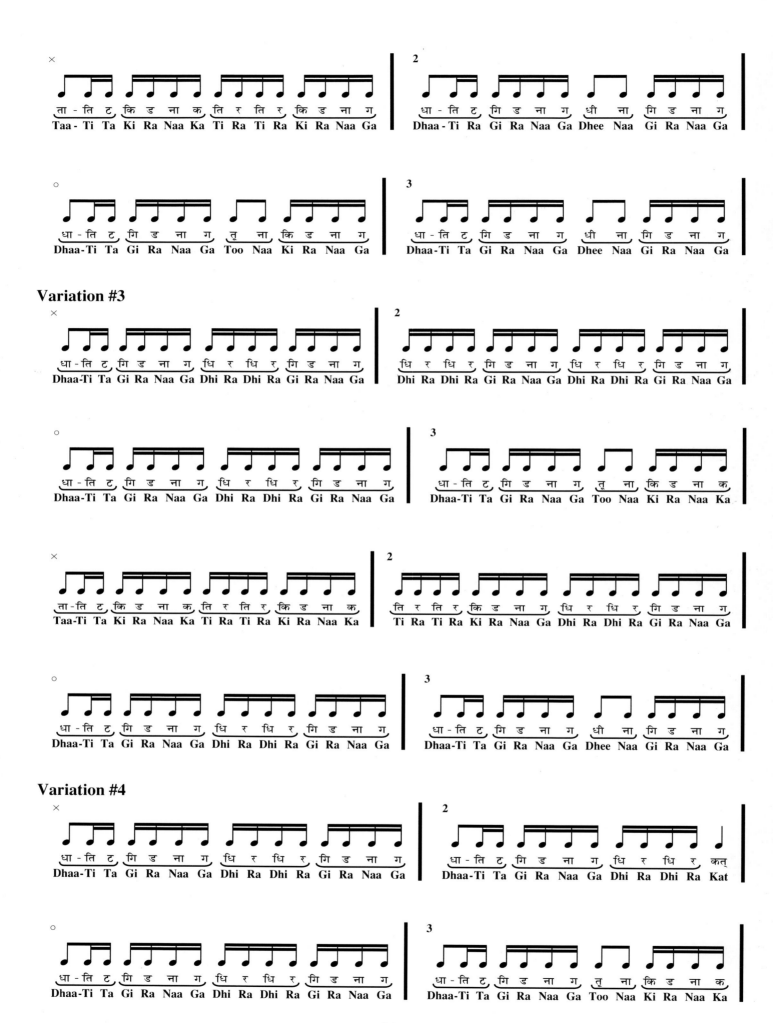

Variation #3

Variation #4

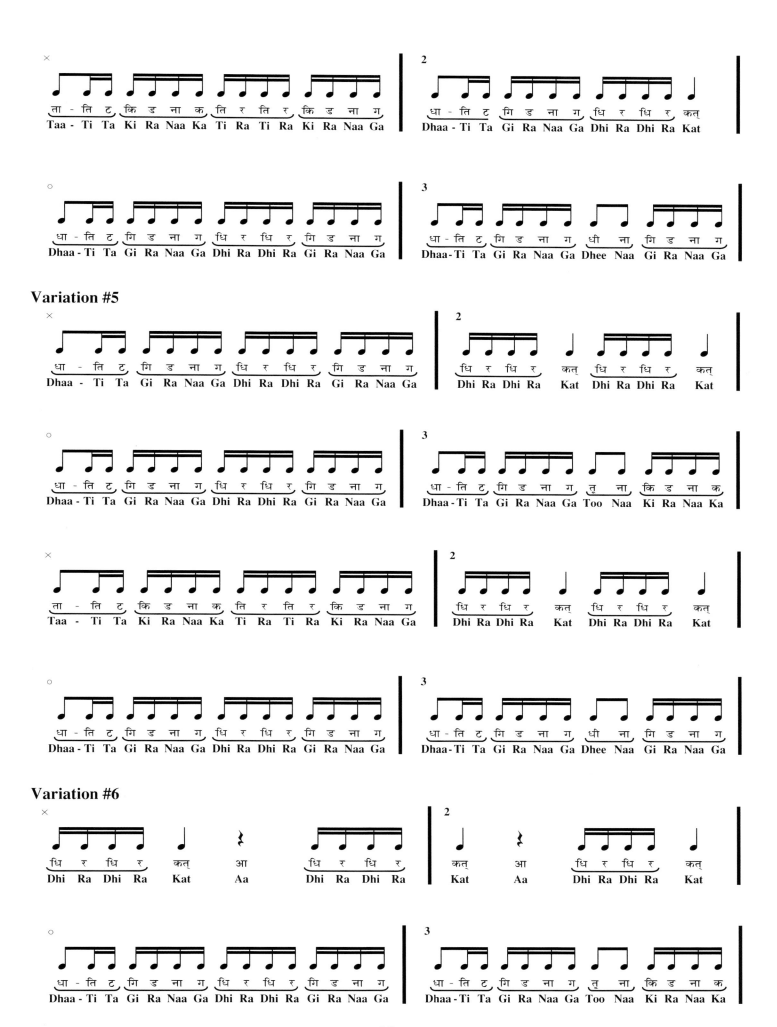

Variation #5

Variation #6

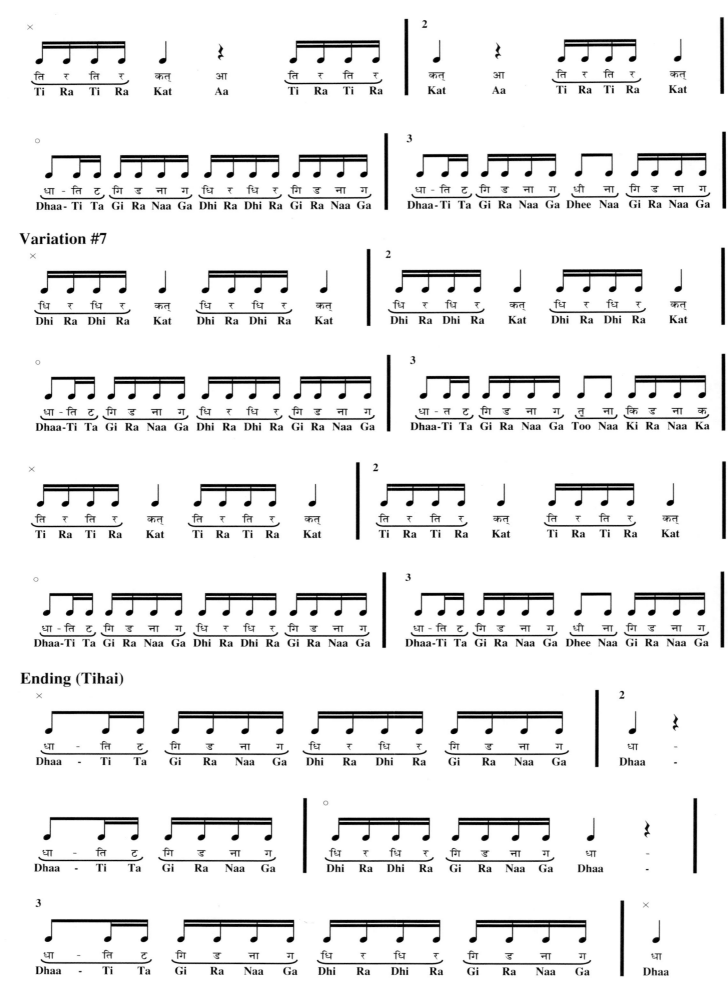

Variation #7

Ending (Tihai)

Please note that the last "Dhaa" of the tihai is the same as the first "Dhaa" of our Tintal theka. The theka continues after the conclusion of the tihai.

SWATANTRA RELA

The swatantra-rela is an extremely common form. The term "swatantra" means "freeform". These relas are almost always loose, improvised performances rather than composed pieces. The unstructured character means that they have virtually no place in the educational process, still we are presenting one here so that you can see how it differs from the kaida-rela.

The following is an interesting example of the swatantra rela. There are a number of bols in this example. Dhaa - Dhaa - TiRaKiTa , Dhaa - TiRaKiTaTaKa, and Dhaa - TiRa KiTaTaKaTiRaKiTa were discussed in the first volume of this series. One may use any technique that is comfortable.

Example 33 - Swatantra Rela in Jhaptal
Variation 1

))) Listen to Track 33 to hear Example 33

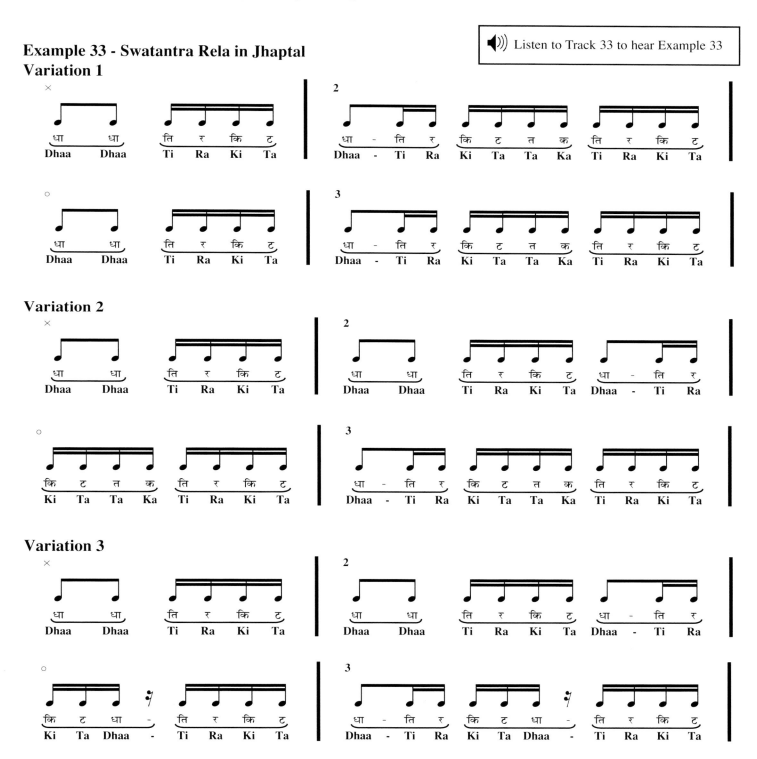

Tihai

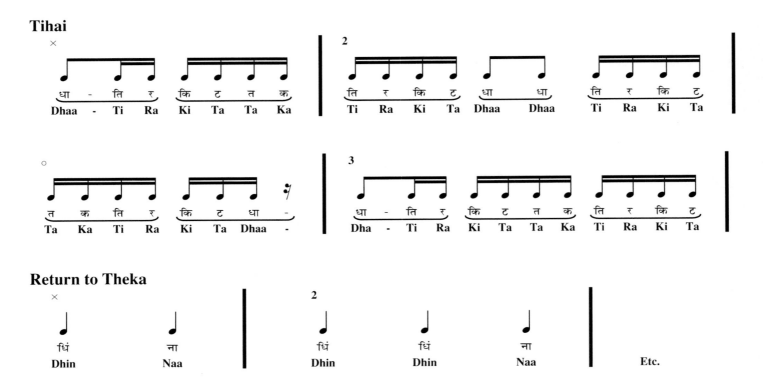

Return to Theka

Let us look at the last example in more detail. We see that there is really no theme as we have come to expect one. It does not conform to any of the rules of kaida. It just sort of flows along until it resolves with a tihai.

The tihai may not jump out at you as being such; but if you look closely, you see that it is based upon the repetition of the phrase:

The timing of this tihai may be a little confusing. The first phrase starts on the beginning of the beat, the second phrase starts half way through the beat, while the last phrase again starts on the beat. It actually makes perfect sense when you hear it; but it looks strange when noted on paper.

SUMMARY

This chapter introduced us to the compositional form known as the rela. We have seen that the key to the rela is speed. Since a rela must be played at very high speeds, this causes the rela to be defined by its function and its bols. Functionally, it allows the tabla player to exert himself/herself and to show their virtuosity. The bol is also a defining factor, because only those bols that may be played at high speeds are suitable.

Structure has no part in defining the rela *per se*; however, we often use the terms kaida-rela or swatantra rela to make statements about its structure and development. A highly structured development of the rela is referred to as a kaida-rela, while an unstructured, freeform approach is referred to as a swatantra-rela.

The designations of kaida versus swatantra must be considered to be end-points of a continuum. In most cases, a rela may have one or more formal characteristics of the kaida, but not enough to be considered a true kaida-rela. Therefore, most relas fall along some midpoint in this continuum according to their depth and structure.

The kaida was introduced in the first book/audio set. It is a highly formalized approach to theme-and-variation; as such, it forms the mainstay of most tabla solos. Let us look at one more.

Here is a famous kaida in Delhi (Dilli) baj. As the name implies, a Delhi technique is to be used throughout. Therefore, Dhaa is standard Delhi style (figure 14), the Ti (ति) is played with the middle finger (figure 6), Ge (गे) is played with the index finger (figure 11), Gin (गिं) is played with two fingers (figure 10) and Ke (के) is the same as Kin (किं) (figure 12) and TiRiKiTa (ति र कि ट) is played as in table 10. If one really wishes to be traditional, the old dilli style, TiRiKiTa (ति र कि ट) may be used (i.e. last stroke as in figure 6).

Example 34 - Delhi Baj Kaida in Tintal

🔊)) Listen to Track 34 to hear Example 34

Theme

Bharan (filler)

39

Variation #1

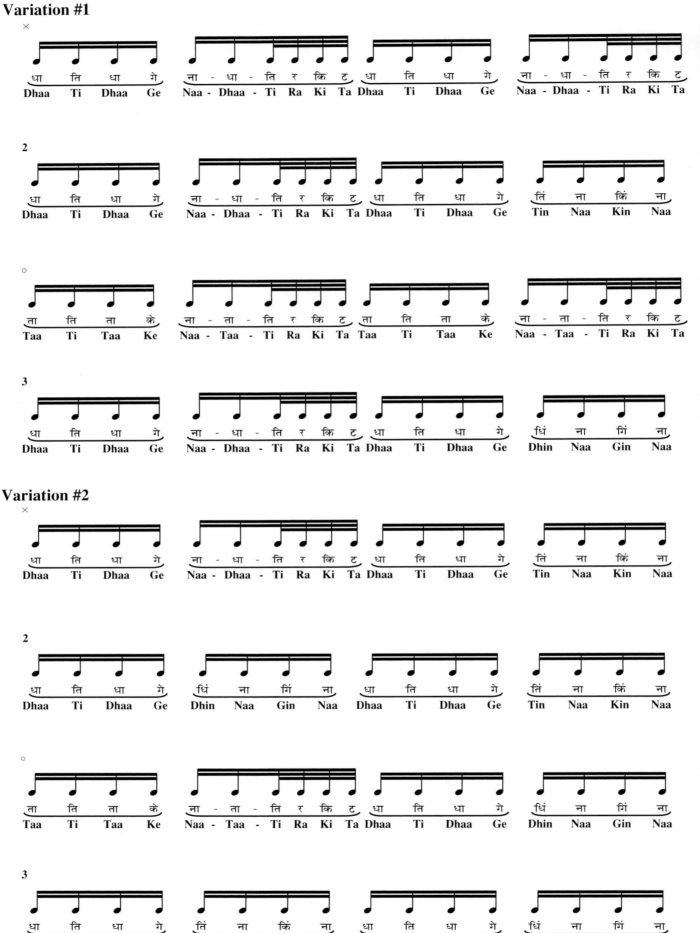

Variation #2

Variation #3

Variation #4

41

Ending (Tihai)

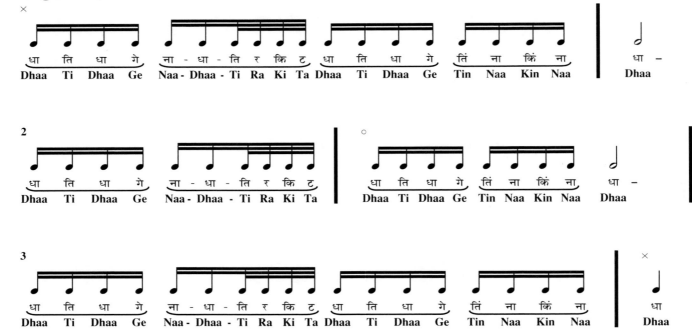

| Dhaa | Ti | Dhaa | Ge | Naa- | Dhaa - | Ti | Ra | Ki | Ta | Dhaa | Ti | Dhaa | Ge | Tin | Naa | Kin | Naa | Dhaa |

SUMMARY

This chapter gave us a new kaida. The kaida is very familiar to us from our first volume; therefore this chapter presented no new concepts for us. However, this is a much more advanced kaida, one that we can present on stage without fear that it is too elementary.

The tabla is not a particularly old instrument. It only came into being about 250-300 years ago. It is very clear that the classical tabla bases much of its tradition, technique, and concepts upon a much older drum; this drum is the pakhawaj.

There is a large body of material that has been transferred from the pakhawaj to the tabla. This chapter will familiarize us with some of this material. However, this material uses techniques and approaches that are different from those we have previously discussed.

Pakhawaj is a two headed barrel drum of the mridang class. For this reason, the pakhawaj is often referred to simply as a "mridang". It is not clear how old the pakhawaj is, but it is safe to say that it is many centuries older than the tabla. There is evidence to suggest that it may even be several thousand years old.

PAKHAWAJ VS. TABLA

It is very useful to compare the structure of the pakhawaj to that of the tabla. By understanding some of the similarities and differences, many issues become clear. The right side of the pakhawaj is usually quite large, generally six to seven inches in diameter. Its construction is very much like a tabla head. The left hand side of the pakhawaj is very different from the tabla (bayan). Instead of there being a permanent black syahi, there is a temporary application of whole wheat flour and water. The fact that this application easily smears makes it very difficult to play this like a tabla.

The dissimilarity in construction between the tabla and the pakhawaj have forced there to be major differences in their respective techniques. It is often difficult to use the same technique for both instruments; but it is possible to make adaptations.

This may clarify the relationship between tabla and pakhawaj technique, but what about the compositions and overall approach? Is there a relationship between these two instruments?

Figure 20. Pakhawaj

There are a lot of conceptual similarities between the tabla and the pakhawaj; this is derived from the fact that for a very long time, tabla players were also pakhawaj players. In the old days, it was the pakhawaj that was considered prestigious, while the tabla had a stigma attached to it. The fact that musicians played both instruments had a great impact upon the style and repertoire of the tabla. To varying degrees, tabla absorbed many elements of the pakhawaj. The Purbi baj is replete with these elements.

This chapter will delve into pakhawaj material that goes beyond the normal Purbi style of playing. We will look at bols and forms that are much closer to the original forms than we have encountered so far.

GENDER ASSOCIATION

There have been gender associations with Indian instruments for a long time. Until the 20th century, the tabla was much associated with female singers and "women's music", while the pakhawaj was greatly associated with masculine forms of singing. Although the tabla has been able to shed its gender associations, the pakhawaj has not. Therefore, whenever one is dealing with pakhawaj material, we must realize that it tends to have a masculine connotation.

How did this gender association come about? It seems that this association came about in Northern India in the 17th-19th centuries. In this period, the men tended to sing in the royal courts while the women tended to sing in the smaller quarters that were often reserved for them. The practical pressures from these very dissimilar environments caused there to be very different approaches to the music and performance. Since the pakhawaj developed its repertoire in the large royal courts where there were no sound systems, they were forced to become very loud. The performances in this environment were often by men. Conversely, the tabla developed its repertoire in the smaller chambers for the accompaniment of women, therefore greater delicacy was encouraged.

NEW BOLS

Before we plunge into the pakhawaj material, there are a few new bols and their techniques that we must learn. We must also remember that these bols may be executed many ways. Therefore, the techniques that are given here should be considered as mere examples, rather than an absolute rule.

TiTaKaTaGaDeeGeNa (ति ट क त ग दी गे न) - This bol, also known as TeTeKaTaGaDeeGeNa (ते टे क त ग दी गे न) is probably the most typical bol found in pakhawaj material. It is used in traditional compositions from all of the gharanas except Delhi (Dilli) and Ajrada. One common technique is shown in table 18. One should note that this bol does not have a complementary form. Therefore, it is ill-suited to bhari/khali structured compositional forms.

Table 18 TiTaKaTaGaDeeGeNa
Ti (ति) - This bol is played with the last three fingers of the right hand in a nonresonant fashion (figure 9).
Ta (ट) - This bol is played with the index finger of the right hand (figure 8).
Ka (क) - Left hand nonresonant slap on the center of the bayan (figure 12)
Ta (त) - Four fingers of the right hand in a nonresonant fashion (figure 5)
Ga (ग) - Standard two-finger Ga (figure 10)
Dee (दी) - Four fingers of right hand in a resonant fashion (figure 21)
Ge (गे) - Standard two-finger Ga (figure 10)
Na (न) - This stroke is variable. For now we will play it with the last three fingers of the right hand in a nonresonant fashion (figure 9).

Figure 21. Dee (दी)

🔊))) Listen to Track 35 to hear Example 35

🔊))) Listen to Track 36 to hear Example 36

Example 35 - Exercise

ति	ट	क	त	ग	दी	गे	न
Ti	Ta	Ka	Ta	Ga	Dee	Ge	Na

Example 36 - Mukhada in Tintal

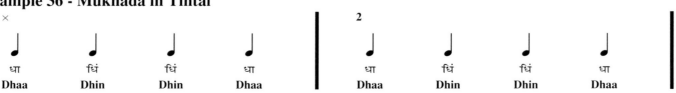

×   2

धा	धिं	धिं	धा	धा	धिं	धिं	धा
Dhaa	Dhin	Dhin	Dhaa	Dhaa	Dhin	Dhin	Dhaa

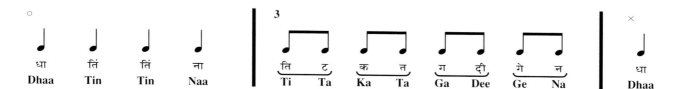

TiRaKiTaTaKaTaa (ति र कि ट त क ता) - This is common bol for both pakhawaj as well as general Purbi compositions. It is powerful, majestic, and easy to play at high speeds. It is very commonly used as a preface to TiTaKaTaGaDeeGeNa (ति ट क त ग दी गे न). The technique is illustrated in table 19.

Table 19 TiRaKiTaTaKaTaa
Ti (ति) - Last three fingers of the right hand in a nonresonant fashion (figure 9)
Ra (र) - Index finger of the right hand (figure 8)
Ki (कि) - Left hand nonresonant slap on the center of the bayan (figure 12)
Ta (ट) - Last three fingers of the right hand in a nonresonant fashion (figure 9)
Ta (त) - This bol is played with the index finger of the right hand (figure 8)
Ka (क) - Left hand nonresonant slap on the center of the bayan (figure 12)
Taa (ता) - Purbi Taa (i.e., similar to a Delhi Tin except played more forcefully) (figure 15)

Example 37 - Exercise

🔊))) Listen to Track 37 to hear Example 37

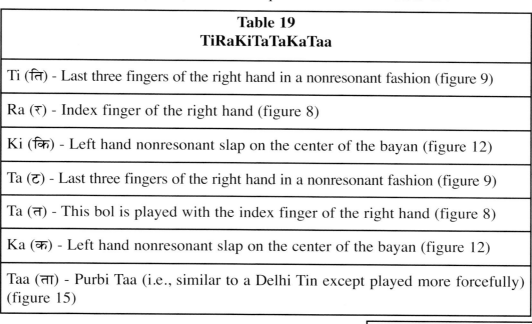

🔊))) Listen to Track 38 to hear Example 38

Example 38 - Mukhada in Tintal

🔊))) Listen to Track 39 to hear Example 39

Example 39 - Simple Mukhada in Tintal

Din (दिं) – Din is conceptually similar to the Dhin of the tabla tradition. However, the execution is somewhat different. For Din (दिं), the right hand strikes the dayan in a resonant fashion with the whole open hand (figure 21). Therefore the index, middle, ring, and little fingers, all strike the dayan at the same time. This right-hand stroke is augmented with a standard Ga of the left hand (figure 10). Here is an exercise for Din (दिं):

Example 40 - Exercise

🔊))) Listen to Track 40 to hear Example 40

Kdaanna (कडान्न) – This is a common bol for pakhawaj compositions. This bol has a complementary form known as Gdaanna (ग्डान्न), but is extremely rare. Furthermore, Kdaanna is seldom used in khali / bhari situations; therefore it may be considered to exist without a complementary form.

The technique is simple; it is a flam with three components. First, the left hand is brought down forcefully as in Ka (figure 12). Immediately afterwards, the last two fingers of the right hand are brought down against the edge of the dayan (figure 4). Finally, a resonant, forceful Purbi Taa (ता) is played (figure 15). One must not forget that this is a flam, therefore all three components need to be executed so close together that they have only a single identity, but not quite simultaneously.

I must point out that there is an alternative technique for Kdaanna. This is exactly the same as the previously mentioned one except there is the addition of a very light foreshadow for the next stroke. This foreshadow is simply a light strike of the dayan with the last two fingers of the right hand (figure 4). Kdaanna is shown in the following exercise:

Example 41 - Exercise

🔊))) Listen to Track 41 to hear Example 41

Ki Ta (कि ट) – This bol was alluded to in the first volume; however it was not discussed in any detail. Although tabla compositions tend to execute KiTa (कि ट) as left hand followed by right hand, pakhawaj compositions tend to execute this entirely with the right hand. This is shown in table 20. One may recognize this technique as being identical to a Purbi TiTa (ति ट).

Table 20 KiTa
Ki (कि) - Last three fingers of the right hand in a nonresonant fashion (figure 9)
Ta (त) - Index finger of the right hand in a nonresonant fashion(figure 8)

Example 42 - Exercise

Ki	Ta	Ki	Ta
किं	ट	किं	ट

OVERVIEW OF TECHNIQUE AND BOLS OF PAKHAWAJ

The bols that we gave in this last section are consistent with the pakhawaj tradition, although the technique has been slightly modified to accommodate the tabla.

There was a minimal adjustment to the technique for the previous bols. Ga (ग), Dhaa (धा) and Taa (ता) are the only bols whose techniques were altered from the original pakhawaj. Even these were done only to accommodate the structural differences between the pakhawaj and the tabla. Other than these, everything else is the same.

The overall conceptualization of these bols may be disorienting for the beginning tabla student. The student is just beginning to get a grasp of the relationship between the bols and the technique, and this chapter changes everything. It is not really as confusing as it seems. The context is what lets us know which of our techniques are implied. Just as we have become used to jumping back and forth between British English and American English, we quickly become accustomed to moving between pakhawaj bols and tabla bols.

PARAN

Paran is a form that is very much associated with the pakhawaj. The term "paran" is obscure, but it appears that it is a corruption of the term "padhant." Padhant is the recitation of bols for a dance performance. It is possible that the parans were compositions that were so beautiful that their bols were suitable for such recitation.

It is difficult to make generalizations about the paran. The only things that we can say with absolute certainty are that the paran is composed of pakhawaj bols, and that it is executed in a technique that is very similar to that of the pakhawaj. There is nothing unique about the structure or usage. Let us look at one elementary example:

Example 43 - Paran in Tintal

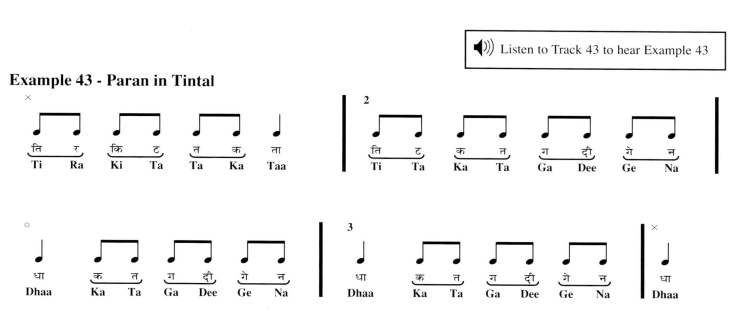

NEW TALS

There are a number of ancient tals which have a very strong association with the pakhawaj. This chapter will deal with four very important ones; Tivra, Chautal, Sool tal and Dhammar. These have been popular for a very long time.

The concept of the "thapi" is linked to the pakhawaj tals. Conceptually, the thapi is almost identical to the concepts of theka or prakar. The differences are largely academic and not significant enough to devote time to them here.

Tivra Tal – Tivra tal is the most popular seven beat tal of the pakhawaj tradition. It is usually considered to be three vibhags of three, two and two matras respectively. All the vibhags are clapped and there are no waves of the hand. Its bols are:

🔊 Listen to Track 44 to hear Example 44

Example 44 - Tivra Tal

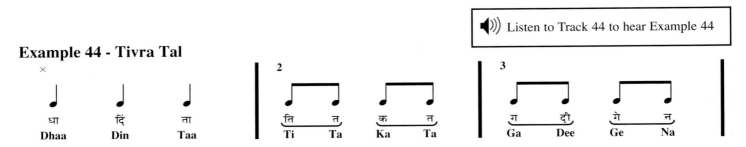

Chautal – Chautal is one of the most popular tals from the old pakhawaj tradition. The name "Chautal" literally means "four-clap" and not surprisingly, it has four claps on its vibhag structure. It is composed of 12 matras; however, there is a lack of agreement concerning the way that the chautal is to be divided. One school suggests that its divisions are the same as Ektal. This would divide it into six vibhags of two matras each. Its clapping arrangement is clap, wave, clap, wave, clap, clap. There is another school of thought which disregards the waves. According to this approach, Chautal is divided into four vibhags. The divisions of the vibhags are four, four, two and two matras respectively. This is the approach that we will be taking in this series. The bols of Chautal are as follows:

🔊 Listen to Track 45 to hear Example 45

Example 45 - Chautal

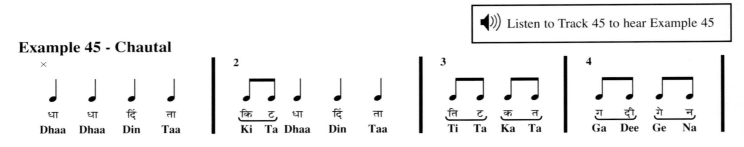

The technique of Chautal is fairly straight forward. Remember that the KiTa (कि ट) is the same as a Purbi TiTa (ति ट) and is executed in the manner shown in table 20. The TiTaKaTaGaDeeGeNa (ति ट क त ग दी गे न) was discussed in table 18.

Sool Tal – Sool tal is an old pakhawaj tal that has been declining in popularity for a number of decades. Still, it is the primary ten beat tal of the old pakhawaj tradition. There is considerable disagreement concerning its bols, vibhag structure, clapping and waving. One common interpretation is shown below:

🔊 Listen to Track 46 to hear Example 46

Example 46 - Sool Tal

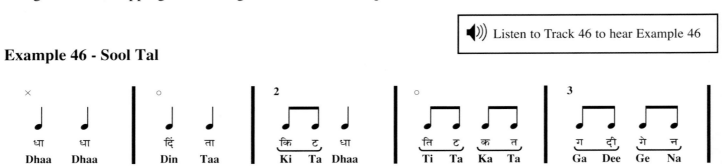

Dhammar Tal – Dhammar is an old tal of 14 matras. It is used to accompany a style of singing which is known as hori or holi. It has four vibhags of five, two, three, and four matras. It has the clapping structure of clap, clap, wave, clap respectively. Its bols are shown below:

Table 21 Dhammar Tal
Kat (कत्) - Left hand slap (figure 12)
Dhee (धी) - last three fingers of right hand (figure 9) with two finger Ga (figure 10)
Ta (ट) - Index finger of right hand in nonresonant strike (figure 8)
Dhee (धी) - last three fingers of right hand (figure 9) with two finger Ga (figure 10)
Ta (ट) - Index finger of right hand in a nonresonant fashion (figure 8)
Dhaa (धा) - Purbi Dhaa (Purbi Taa as in figure 15 with two finger bayan in figure 10)
Ga (ग) - Two-finger Ga (figure 10)
Tee (ती) - Last three fingers of right hand (figure 9)
Ta (ट) - Index finger of right hand in nonresonant fashion (figure 8)
Tee (ती) - Last three fingers of right hand (figure 9)
Ta (ट) - Index finger of right hand in nonresonant fashion (figure 8)
Taa (ता) - Purbi Taa (figure 15)

◀))) Listen to Track 47 to hear Example 47

Example 47 - Dhammar Tal

कत्	धी	ट	धी	ट	धा	-	ग	ती	ट	ती	ट	ता	-
Kat	Dhee	Ta	Dhee	Ta	Dhaa	-	Ga	Tee	Ta	Tee	Ta	Taa	-

SUMMARY

This pakhawaj material introduced a number of interesting and different twists to the performance of tabla. The new bols, new techniques, and new concepts, may be a little disconcerting to the student the first time that they are encountered. However with diligent practice, this material greatly broadens the performance possibilities.

MORE TALS
& PRAKARS

This chapter will allow us to cover new tals as well as prakars of tals that were covered in the first volume. As was mentioned earlier, the tals and their associated thekas, are the fundamental rhythmic forms behind Indian music. The prakars are the different approaches to playing them.

ULTRA-FAST TINTAL PRAKAR

Tintal may be performed in extremely fast tempos. We have already discussed some fast prakars in our chapter on alternative techniques. At that time, one may have thought that these covered all cases; sadly this is not the case. There is a style known as jhaala which is commonly used by instrumentalists (sitar, sarod, santur, etc.) that requires us to play at even higher speeds. Below are some Tintal prakars that work well for these situations:

🔊))) Listen to Track 48 to hear Example 48

Example 48
Ultra-Fast Tintal Prakar

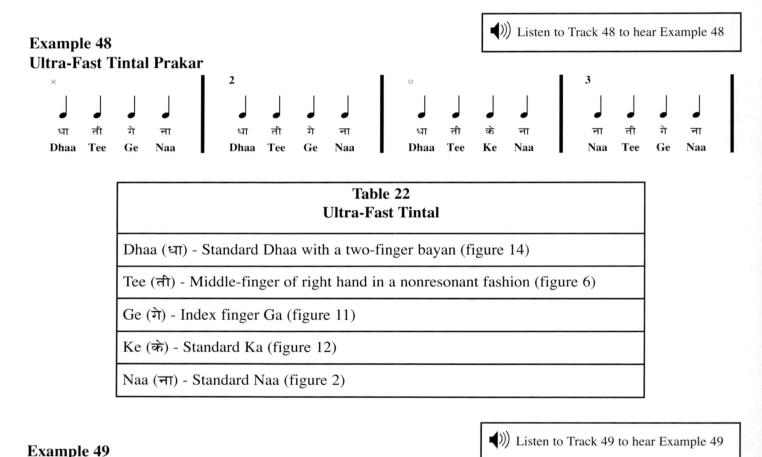

धा	ती	गे	ना	धा	ती	गे	ना	धा	ती	के	ना	ना	ती	गे	ना
Dhaa	Tee	Ge	Naa	Dhaa	Tee	Ge	Naa	Dhaa	Tee	Ke	Naa	Naa	Tee	Ge	Naa

Table 22
Ultra-Fast Tintal
Dhaa (धा) - Standard Dhaa with a two-finger bayan (figure 14)
Tee (ती) - Middle-finger of right hand in a nonresonant fashion (figure 6)
Ge (गे) - Index finger Ga (figure 11)
Ke (के) - Standard Ka (figure 12)
Naa (ना) - Standard Naa (figure 2)

🔊))) Listen to Track 49 to hear Example 49

Example 49
Ultra-Fast Tintal Prakar

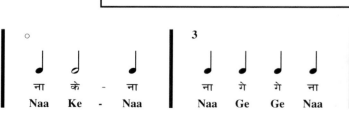

ना	गे	गे	ना	ना	गे	गे	ना	ना	के	-	ना	ना	गे	गे	ना
Naa	Ge	Ge	Naa	Naa	Ge	Ge	Naa	Naa	Ke	-	Naa	Naa	Ge	Ge	Naa

DADRA PRAKAR

Here is a prakar of Dadra tal. One will notice that this is the same approach and same concept as the example that was shown in example 29. However, where the earlier example used a nonstandard technique, this one uses a standard technique.

Example 50 - Dadra Tal Prakar

Listen to Track 50 to hear Example 50

JHAPTAL PRAKAR

Here is prakar of Jhaptal. This prakar illustrates an interesting process. Notice that the second and the fourth vibhags have been constructed by taking the normal Dhin Dhin Naa and playing them twice at double speed. It is very easy to remember that any phrase may be played twice at double speed, because the timing will always be the same!

Listen to Track 51 to hear Example 51

Example 51 - Jhaptal Prakar

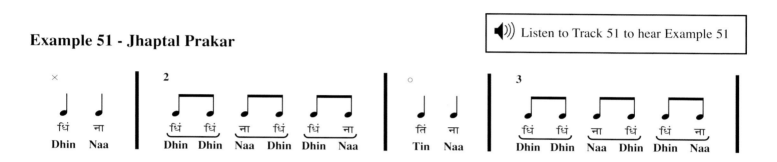

RUPAK PRAKAR

Here is a prakar of Rupak tal. Notice that the last two vibhags illustrate the same process that was shown in example 51.

Listen to Track 52 to hear Example 52

Example 52 - Rupak Tal Prakar

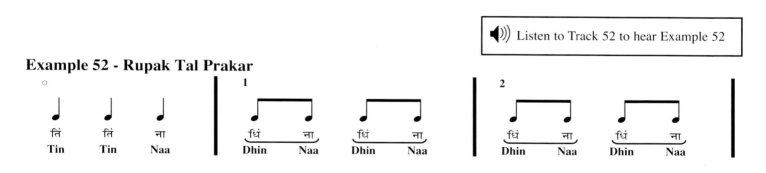

DIPCHANDI PRAKAR

Here is a prakar of Dipchandi which is very popular. Although the bols are very different from the Dipchandi that was shown in the first volume, this version has been made popular by its usage in film songs and other lighter forms of music. Please note that the last two Naas are augmented with a Ka.

Listen to Track 53 to hear Example 53

Example 53 - Dipchandi Prakar

KAHERAVA PRAKARS

It is likely that no other tal has as many prakars as Kaherava. This is because virtually any four, eight or 16 beat tal from the nonclassical traditions tends to be lumped under this heading. Here are two more prakars that one can work with:

Bhajan ka Theka - This is one of the most popular prakars in India. As its name indicates, it is used to accompany the Hindu religious songs known as bhajan. In theory, this tal is an eight beat tal; however, for simplicity sake, we are noting it as though it were a very fast 16 beat tal. The technique is straight forward, except for the Gas at the end of each vibhag; these should be played with the index finger (figure 11).

))) Listen to Track 54 to hear Example 54

Example 54 - Kaherava Prakar (Bhajan ka Theka)

Filmi Prakar - This prakar has been popularized by the Hindi film industry. It is very simple and has a nice feel to it. This prakar is a good example of how far the prakars of Kaherava can deviate from the "official" version. This prakar is clearly four beats, where the generally accepted version of Kaherava has eight beats. Furthermore, the bols have almost no relationship to the "textbook" Kaherava. Still, the popularity of this prakar means that it cannot be dismissed.

Example 55 - Kaherava Filmi Prakar

))) Listen to Track 55 to hear Example 55

TILWADA

Tilwada tal is composed of 16 beats. Like Tintal, it is four vibhags of four matras each, with a clapping arrangement of clap, clap, wave, clap. Although the overall structure is identical to Tintal, it does have a different theka. Its theka is as follows:

))) Listen to Track 56 to hear Example 56

Example 56 - Tilwada Tal

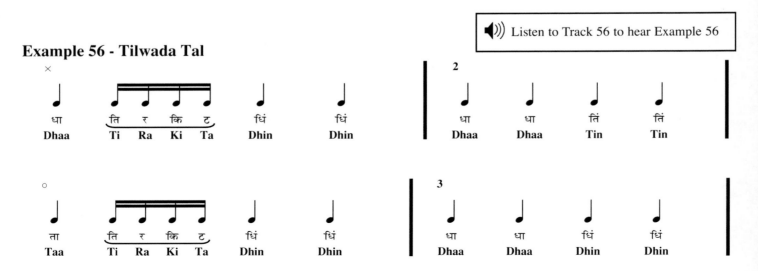

JHOOMRA

Jhoomra tal is a fourteen beat pattern that is sometimes used to accompany classical vocal styles. It is structured very much like Dipchandi. It has four vibhags of three, four, three, and four matras. These vibhags are denoted with a clap, clap, wave, and clap respectively. The theka is shown below:

Listen to Track 57 to hear Example 57

Example 57 - Jhoomra Tal

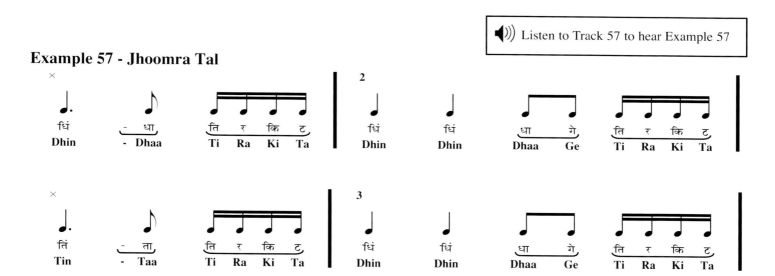

SUMMARY

This chapter gave us several new things. We learned a few new prakars of tals; these tals were introduced in the first volume. We also learned a few new tals that were not discussed earlier. Although there are no new concepts, this is still important material that must be part of our repertoire.

TRANSITIONS

This chapter deals with the manner in which technique changes as we move from one bol expression to another. This addresses a very common problem. Various bols and bol expressions are normally strung together to create larger compositions. One expression may end in a way that the hand is not well positioned to execute the next bol. The way to get around this awkwardness is simple; one either alters the end of the first bol expression, or one alters the beginning of the second expression. This alteration is done in such away as to make the transitions between the two expressions easy and seamless. This will be the topic of this chapter.

These transitions have an interesting effect upon the way that we look at bols. It creates a situation where the initial and the final syllable of these expressions become inherently ambiguous. Their technique becomes dependent upon the context of the bol expression.

TIRAKITATAKA

TiRaKiTaTaKa (ति र कि ट त क) is a common bol expressions of tabla; it was introduced in the first book/audio set. It displays ambiguity in both the initial as well as the final stroke. We will give several examples to illustrate this point.

<table>
<tr><td>◀))) Listen to Track 58 to hear Example 58</td></tr>
</table>

Example 58 - Exercise

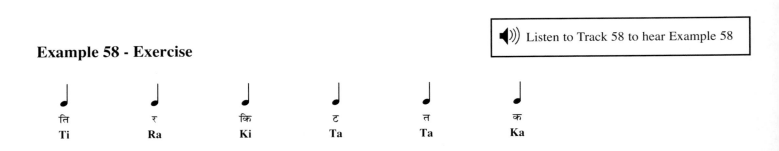

ति	र	कि	ट	त	क
Ti	Ra	Ki	Ta	Ta	Ka

Table 23
TiRaKiTaTaKa (Transition #1)
Ti (ति) - Ti is a transitional bol. In exercise 58, it is most easily executed in a Purbi fashion. This is where the last three fingers of the right hand are used to strike the dayan in a nonresonant fashion (figure 9)
Ra (र) - Index finger in dayan in nonresonant fashion (figure 8)
Ki (कि) - Left hand nonresonant (i.e., Ka) (figure 12)
Ta (ट) - Last three fingers of the right hand are used to strike the dayan in a nonresonant fashion (figure 9)
Ta (त) - Index finger in dayan in nonresonant fashion (figure 8)
Ka (क) - Left hand nonresonant (i.e., Ka) (figure 12)

It is very interesting to look at the last exercise. Its technique is described in table 23. If we look at the transition between the TiRaKiTa (ति र क ट) and the TaKa (त क) we see that the final Ta (ट) is most easily executed in a pure Purbi style (i.e., three fingers of right hand shown in figure 9). The transition as it turns back around for a repetition shows the same thing; the initial Ti (ति) is most easily executed in a Purbi style (i.e., last three fingers of right hand shown in figure 9).

Let us look at a usage of TiRaKiTa that shows a different set of hand movements.

Example 59 - Exercise

🔊))) Listen to Track 59 to hear Example 59

धा	-	ति	र	कि	ट	त	क
Dhaa	-	Ti	Ra	Ki	Ta	Ta	Ka

The last exercise shows how the flow of the technique has been drastically altered by the modification of two strokes. Its technique is described in table 24. Although it is certainly possible to execute the TiRaKiTaTaKa with the technique of the earlier example (i.e., the initial Purbi Ti (ति) as well as the final Ka (क)), we find that the technique may be made more efficient by altering both the initial Ti (ति) as well as the last Ka (क). For this, let us execute the initial Ti (ति) using the Delhi technique (i.e., middle finger-figure 6) and the last Ka with the index finger of the left hand (similar to a index-finger Ga but nonresonant - figure 11).

Table 24
TiRaKiTaTaKa (Transition #2)
Ti (ति) - Ti is a transitional bol. In the preceding exercise it is most easily executed in a Delhi fashion. This is where the middle finger of the right hand is used to strike the dayan in a nonresonant fashion (figure 6)
Ra (र) - No change (figure 8)
Ki (कि) - No change (figure 12)
Ta (ट) - No change (figure 9)
Ta (त) - No change (figure 8)
Ka (क) - This is a transitional bol. Within this context it is more easily executed with the index finger of the left hand in a manner which is somewhat remeniscent of a one finger Ga (ग) (figure 11)

TITAKATAGADEEGENA

TiTaKaTaGaDeeGeNa (ति ट क त ग दी गे न) is bol that was introduced in an earlier chapter and is a good example of the use of transitional techniques. Let us review the previously given exercise but this time with a slightly different technique.

Example 60 - Exercise

🔊))) Listen to Track 60 to hear Example 60

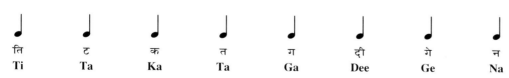

ति	ट	क	त	ग	दी	गे	न
Ti	Ta	Ka	Ta	Ga	Dee	Ge	Na

Let us examine the technique laid out in table 25. We see that the original technique described in table 18 was very awkward when we tried to loop TiTaKaTaGaDeeGeNa around and repeat it. The basic problem came from a repetition of the last three fingers of the right hand. However, by incorporating a Delhi approach for the first and last strokes, the technique suddenly becomes much more efficient and much faster.

Table 25
TiTaKaTaGaDeeGeNa (Transition #1)
Ti (ति) - This bol is a transitional bol. For this exercise play it with the middle finger of the right hand. (figure 6)
Ta (ट) - This bol is played with the index finger of the right hand. (figure 8)
Ka (क) - Left hand nonresonant slap on the center of the bayan (figure 12)
Ta (त) - Four fingers of the right hand in a nonresonant fashion (figure 5)
Ga (ग) - Standard Ga (figure 10)
Dee (दी) - Four fingers of right hand in a resonant fashion (figure 21)
Ge (गे) - Standard two-finger Ga (figure 10)
Na (न) - This stroke is transitional. For this exercise play it with the last two fingers of the right hand in a non-resonant fashion. (figure 4)

Let us look at another approach towards handling transitions in TiTaKaTaGaDeeGeNa. For this let us look at the exercise in example 61.

🔊))) Listen to Track 61 to hear Example 61

Example 61 - Exercise

धा	-	ति	ट	क	त	ग	दी	गे	न
Dhaa	-	Ti	Ta	Ka	Ta	Ga	Dee	Ge	Na

The technique for this example is shown in table 26. We see that the initial three finger Ti (ति) does not need to be altered from our standard technique (table 18). However, there is a slight inefficiency in the last stroke. If we attempt to execute example 61 with the technique originally described in table 18, we find that we are forced to reposition our hand as we move from the last Na (न) back around to start another Dhaa (धा). If we play this exercise using the technique shown in table 25 then we see that no repositioning of the hands is necessary. The last Na (न) is played in such a way that it leaves us in our home position.

Table 26 **TiTaKaTaGaDeeGeNa (Transition #2)**
Ti (ति) - This is a transitional bol. For this exercise, play it with the last three fingers of the right hand. (figure 9)
Ta (ट) - Same technique as before (see table 25).
Ka (क) - Same technique as before (see table 25).
Ta (त) - Same technique as before (see table 25).
Ga (ग) - Same technique as before (see table 25).
Dee (दी) - Same technique as before (see table 25).
Ge (गे) - Same technique as before (see table 25).
Na (न) - This stroke is transitional. For this exercise play it with the last two fingers of the right hand in a non-resonant fashion as we did in the preceding exercise (figure 4).

SUMMARY

This chapter acquainted us with the subject of transitional techniques. We saw that the beginning and final stroke of any bol expression should be considered to be ambiguous as to how it is played. Their technique is subject to change according to the bols which come before the expression and those which come after it.

I will give one piece of advice concerning the level of ambiguity of these techniques. As you progress through your studies, you will find that the last stroke of a bol expression is highly variable while the first stroke is rarely variable.

This chapter was just a brief introduction to transitional techniques. We did not even cover all of the possible transitions involved in TiTaKaTaGaDeeGeNa or TiRaKiTaTaKa, much less the myriad of other bol expressions. However with this brief introduction, future references to the subject should not be confusing or surprising.

MORE TIHAIS & CHAKRADARS

The tihai and the chakradar are probably the two most common forms of cadence for the tabla. Their concept is not too difficult, but the execution is at times quite challenging.

The tihai is a very simple cadence. It is a phrase that is repeated three times. Although it may begin at any point in the cycle, it usually ends upon the sam (first beat of the cycle). The tihai was introduced in the first volume of this series; but there has not been much discussion about it.

The chakradar is basically a tihai in which each phrase itself contains a tihai. This will become clear as we move along in this chapter.

TIHAI

The tihai is very common, but it is not intuitive to the the non-Indian musician. One reason for its inaccessibility lies in the mathematics of its execution. This peculiarity stems from the fact that the last beat of the tihai overlaps with the first beat of the next cycle. For example, Tintal tihais may be 17 matras, 33 matras, 49 matras, 65 matras, etc., while ordinary Tintal compositions will normally contain 16 matras, 32 matras, 48 matras, 64 matras, etc.

There are two basic forms of tihai. These are distinguished by the presence or absence of pauses between the phrases. Whenever a tihai has these pauses, it is referred to as a "damdar" tihai; whenever the pauses are absent, then the tihai is said to be "bedam".

Damdar Tihai - The term damdar is interesting. There are two parts to the word; there is the "dam" and the "dar". The word "dam" literally means "breath", but this does not mean that it is a tihai that "breathes". Instead the word "dam" has acquired a secondary meaning in Hindi / Urdu for a very small interval of time. The suffix "dar", means "something, or someone who has, or has the qualities of something." Therefore, the term "damdar" implies a tihai which contains small pauses in it. The structure of the damdar tihai is shown in figure 22.

Here are a few damdar tihais:

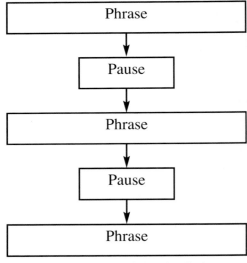

Figure 22. Structure of damdar tihai

Example 62 - Damdar Tihai in Tintal

Listen to Track 62 to hear Example 62

धा	तिं	तिं	ना
Dhaa	**Tin**	**Tin**	**Naa**

3

ति	र	कि	ट	धा	-	ति	र	कि	ट	धा	-	ति	ट	कि	ट	धा
Ti	**Ra**	**Ki**	**Ta**	**Dhaa**	-	**Ti**	**Ra**	**Ki**	**Ta**	**Dhaa**	-	**Ti**	**Ta**	**Ki**	**Ta**	**Dhaa**

Listen to Track 63 to hear Example 63

Example 63 - Damdar Tihai in Tintal

धा	धिं	धिं	धा	धा	धिं	धिं	धा
Dhaa	**Dhin**	**Dhin**	**Dhaa**	**Dhaa**	**Dhin**	**Dhin**	**Dhaa**

ति	र	कि	ट	धा	ति	र	कि	ट	धा	ति	र	कि	ट	धा
Ti	**Ra**	**Ki**	**Ta**	**Dhaa**	**Ti**	**Ra**	**Ki**	**Ta**	**Dhaa**	**Ti**	**Ra**	**Ki**	**Ta**	**Dhaa**

Listen to Track 64 to hear Example 64

Example 64 - Damdar Tihai in Tintal

ति	र	कि	ट	धा	धा	धा	-	ति	र	कि	ट
Ti	**Ra**	**Ki**	**Ta**	**Dhaa**	**Dhaa**	**Dhaa**	-	**Ti**	**Ra**	**Ki**	**Ta**

धा	धा	धा	-	ति	र	कि	ट	धा	धा	धा
Dhaa	**Dhaa**	**Dhaa**	-	**Ti**	**Ra**	**Ki**	**Ta**	**Dhaa**	**Dhaa**	**Dhaa**

Listen to Track 65 to hear Example 65

Example 65 - Damdar Tihai in Tintal

ति	ट	क	त	ग	दी	गे	न	धा	-	ति	ट	क	त
Ti	**Ta**	**Ka**	**Ta**	**Ga**	**Dee**	**Ge**	**Na**	**Dhaa**	-	**Ti**	**Ta**	**Ka**	**Ta**

ग	दी	गे	न	धा	-	ति	ट	क	त	ग	दी	गे	न	धा
Ga	**Dee**	**Ge**	**Na**	**Dhaa**	-	**Ti**	**Ta**	**Ka**	**Ta**	**Ga**	**Dee**	**Ge**	**Na**	**Dhaa**

 Listen to Track 66 to hear Example 66

Example 66 - Damdar Tihai in Tintal

Bedam Tihai - The bedam tihai is also a common form of tihai. The name "bedam", literally means a "without pause" (remember that "dam" may mean either a "breath" or "a small unit of time"). As the name implies, the bedam tihai does not have any pauses separating the three phrases. Its structure is diagrammatically shown in figure 23.

Here are a few easy bedam tihais:

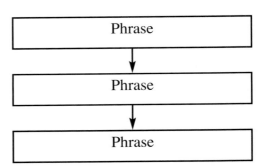

Figure 23. Structure of bedam tihai

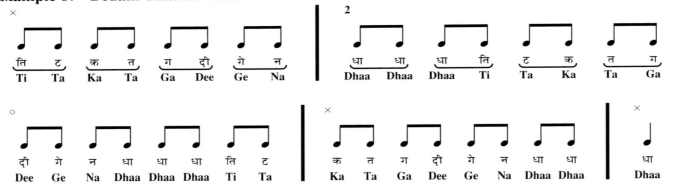 Listen to Track 67 to hear Example 67

Example 67 - Bedam Tihai in Tintal

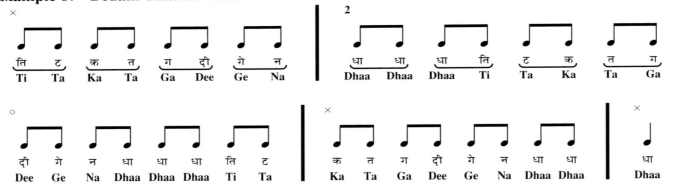

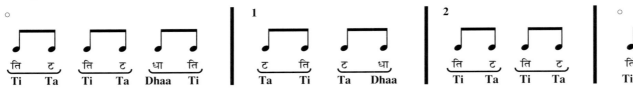 Listen to Track 68 to hear Example 68

Example 68 - Bedam Tihai in Rupak Tal

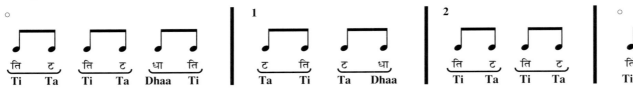

60

CHAKRADAR

The chakradar is a type of tihai in which each phrase contains a tihai. There are a number of structures which fulfil this requirement; but for this volume we will only deal with one.

The bols used in the chakradar in example 69 have all been given earlier. DhiRaDhiRa (धि र धि र) is found in table 2. KiTaTaKa (कि ट त क) may not have been seen in this particular context, but it is fairly intuitive; it is nothing but the left hand (क) (figure 12), last three fingers of right hand (figure 9), index finger of right hand (figure 8), and left hand (क)(figure 12). Taa (ता) is in the Purbi style (figure 15), and Kdaana (कडान्न) was described in the exercise in example 41.

🔊)) Listen to Track 69 to hear Example 69

Example 69 - Chakradar in Tintal

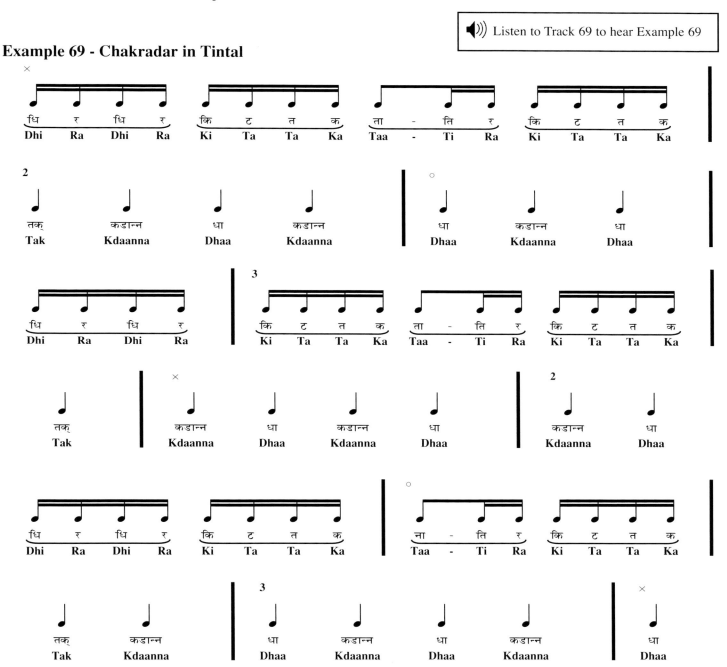

The structure of the previous chakradar deserves some discussion. We see in the last example that the phrase Kdaanna Dhaa is repeated nine times. This is what makes it a chakradar.

SUMMARY

This chapter discussed the tihai and the chakradar. The tihai was introduced in our first volume, but greatly expanded upon here. The chakradar is essentially a tihai based upon smaller tihais; this is a new topic. Although the chakradar is an important subject in north Indian music, we must content ourselves with but a short introduction here.

GAT

The gat is a very common, yet ambiguously defined compositional form. It was given its present importance by the Lucknow, Farukhabad and Benares traditions, yet today it is played by musicians from all over India.

Gats are the cornerstone of solo performances for many artists. Although they are fixed compositions, one may string gats together in a fashion that makes them flexible enough for both tabla solos as well as the solo portions of accompaniment situations. One can even mix precomposed gats with improvisation for an interesting effect.

There are frequent disagreements as to theoretical aspects of the gat. We can say with certainty that it is played in a Purbi style. We can also say that it is a fully precomposed form as opposed to an improvisation. Beyond that, we cannot say anything without getting into debates (sometimes acrimonious) with many musicians who have more definite views on the subject.

The various opinions as to the exact definition of gat have some interesting ramifications. Some gats have only a single structure. Some gats have two structures (khali and bhari as found in kaidas). Some gats have three sections; some have four sections.

We will not even attempt to address these numerous, and often conflicting views in this modest work. We will simply give an introductory example.

HAJI SAHIB GAT

This is a gat that is said to have been composed by Vilayal Ali Khan. His *nom de plume* was Haji Sahib, which is in reference to his trips to Makka (Mecca); in Islam, one who makes this pilgrimage assumes the title of "Haji".

The technique is fairly straight forward. It is a standard Purbi technique. The bol Tak (तक्) is played with the right hand as shown in figure 5. There are two opinions as to how the phrase Tak - KiTa (तक् - कि ट) should be played. One school has the beat divided into four units such that it is 8th-note, 16th, 16th; this is the approach that is shown here. However, another school suggests that this phrase should be played in triplets. For simplicity sake, we are showing the version that is played in quadruple time.

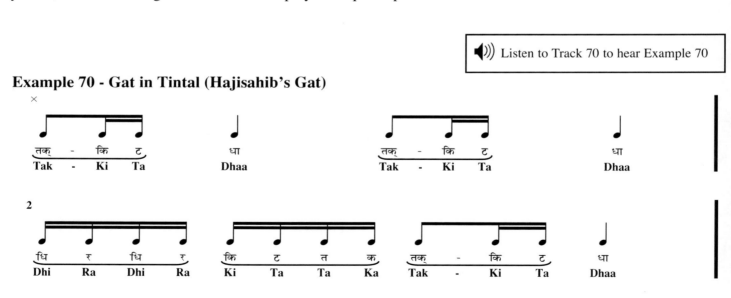

◀))) Listen to Track 70 to hear Example 70

Example 70 - Gat in Tintal (Hajisahib's Gat)

Let us make a few comments concerning the performance of this gat. Unlike kaida, there is no need to first play it slowly and then play it fast. Furthermore, there may be a variation or two added to this gat, but it is certainly not obligatory. It is customary to close this with a tihai. A good example would be to play the chakradar shown in example 69 to bring this to a close.

SUMMARY

The topic of the gat is central to many of the Eastern (Purbi) approaches to the tabla. Even today, it is an important part of the repertoire of musicians from the Lucknow, Benares, and Farukhabad traditions. Unfortunately, we can only make the briefest introduction to this form here.

LAGGI

Laggis and their associated pickups are very common in lighter nonclassical styles of music. We get a very brief introduction to this form in this chapter.

The laggi is an improvised assertion on the part of the tabla player. It tends to be very loose and unstructured. This is in contrast to the highly structured format of the kaida.

The pickup is a small flourish which may be used either at the start of the laggi or the finish. It is a transitional device which may be similar to the mukhada or the tihai. It is also referd to as a turnaround or even by the Hindi/Urdu "toda".

Let us take a very simple example. In this example we will string a theka, a pickup, several laggis, a tihai and then return to the theka.

🔊 Listen to Track 71 to hear Example 71

Example 71
(laggi in Kaherava with pickup and tihai)

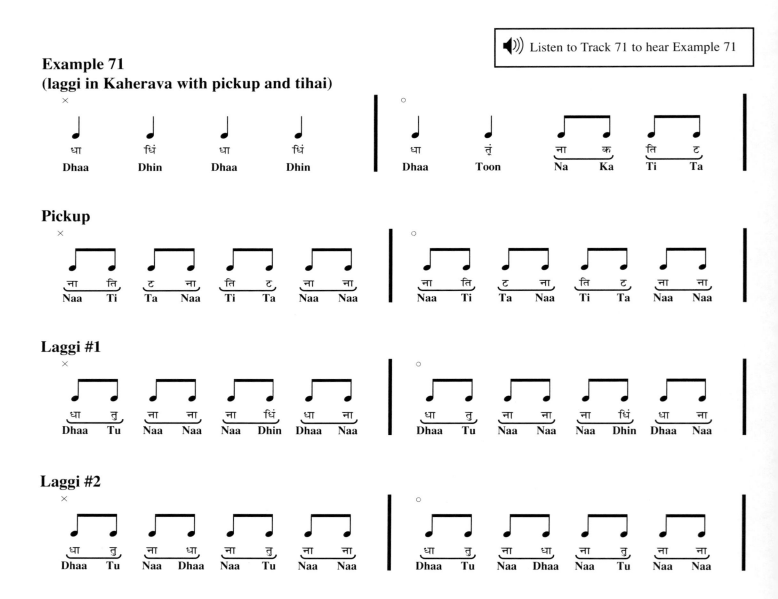

Laggi #3

| Dhaa | Tu | Naa - Ki Naa | Naa | Dhin | Dhaa | Naa | | Dhaa | Tu | Naa - Ki Naa | Naa | Dhin | Dhaa | Naa |

Tihai

| Dhaa | Tu | Naa | Naa | Dhaa | Dhaa | Tu | | Naa | Naa | Dhaa | Dhaa | Tu | Naa | Naa | | Dhaa |

Table 27
NaaTiTaNaaTiTaNaaNaa
Naa (ना) - Standard Naa (figure 2) augmented with a Ka (figure 12)
Ti (ति) - Purbi style (last three fingers on syahi) (figure 9)
Ta (ट) - Index finger in syahi (figure 8)
Naa (ना) - Standard Naa (figure 2) augmented with a Ka (figure 12)
Ti (ति) - Purbi style (last three fingers on syahi) (figure 9)
Ta (ट) - Index finger in syahi (figure 8)
Naa (ना) - Standard Naa (figure 2) augmented with a Ka (figure 12)
Naa (ना) - Standard Naa (figure 2)

The technique of this last laggi is fairly intuitive. There really should be no need to discuss it at length.

This Kaherava prakar was discussed in the first volume of this series. If you have any questions concerning it, please review the appropriate material.

The pickup is fairly self explanatory. There is one point to keep in mind; within this pickup, all of the Naas (ना) are augmented with a Ka (क) except the last one. This is described in table 27.

SUMMARY
The laggi is the foundation for the lighter forms of improvisation. However, the inherently free-form nature of these improvisations makes it difficult to pin down. Still, this simple example gives us a small taste of this style.

CONCLUSION

This finishes up the second set of "Learning the Tabla". You have gone a considerable distance from where you left off in the first set. But you may be asking yourself, "Where do I go from here?" Here are a few ideas.

I recommend practice - more practice—a lot of practice! Practice the material with the audio. Practice the material without the audio. Get together with people, and try your hand at accompaniment. Find people who are skilled at traditional Indian instrumental and vocal forms, and practice the traditional material.

Get more material! There is undoubtedly more material that you can get from your teacher. There are also numerous books that can give you more material. The internet is a good place to find these other resources.

Practice and study are certainly going to be your top priority at this time; but in the final analysis, it is all about the music. We have all seen people who have learned for decades and have become technically very proficient. They may be able to play compositions with perfection; however, if the compositions are devoid of life, it amounts to nothing. Parroting back compositions may demonstrate ones training and technical proficiency, but it does not guarantee a beautiful performance.

In this world there are artists and there are technicians, which one are you going to become?

The key to becoming an artist lies within yourself. Nothing and no one else can bring this forth. Although, the path to technical proficiency is very clear, there is no reliable roadmap to becoming an artist. It is only with time, experimentation, and a lot of introspection, that you may be able to nurture that aesthetic fire within you.

Good luck!

APPENDIX

Variations in Bol

Below is a chart that shows the variation in many of the common bols of tabla.

Variations in Bol for Common Techniques
TiRaKiTa (ति र कि ट), TiRaKaTa (ति र क ट), TiRiKiTa (ति रि कि ट), TiRaKeeTa (ति र की ट), TaRiKeeTa (ता रि की ट)
TeTe (ते टे), TiTa (ति ट), TeTa (ते ट)
TiTaGiDaNaGa (ति ट गि ड न ग), TeTeGiDaNaGa (ते टे गि ड न ग), TeTeGiRaNaGa (ते टे गि ड न ग), TiTaGiDaNaaGa (ति ट गि ड ना ग), TeTeGiDaNaaGa (ते टे गि ड ना ग), TeTeGiRaNaaGa (ते टे गि ड ना ग)
Dhin (धिं), Dheen (धीं), Dhee (धी), Dhi (धि)
Naa (ना), Taa (ता)
Dhaa (धा), Dha (ध)
GiRaNaaGa (गि ड ना ग), GiDaNaaGa (गि ड ना ग), GeRaNaaGa (गे ड ना ग), GheDaNaaGa (घे ड ना ग), GhiDaNaaGa (घि ड ना ग)
KiRaNaaKa (कि ड ना क), KiDaNaaKa (कि ड ना क), KiRaNaKa (कि ड न क), KiDaNaKa (कि ड न क), KeRaNaaKa (के ड ना क), KeDaNaaKa (कि ड ना क)
Tun (तुं), Toon (तूं), Thun (थुं), Thoon (थूं), Tu (तु), Too (तू), Thu (थु), Thoo (थू)
Ka (क), Ke (के), Ki (कि), Kin (किं), Kee (की), Kat (कत्)
TiTaKaTaGaDeeGeNa (ति ट क त ग दी गे न), TeTeKaTaGaDeeGeNa (ते टे क त ग दी गे न), TeTaKaTaGaDeeGeNa (ते ट क त ग दी गे न), TiTaKaTaGaDiGeNa (ति ट क त ग दि गे न), TeTeKaTaGaDiGeNa (ते टे क त ग दि गे न)

67

David Courtney has been involved in Indian music since the early 70's. In 1972, he had a radio program on KPFT - Houston, entitled "Evening Ragas". In 1975 he moved to California and studied pakhawaj under the famous Zakir Hussain at the Ali Akbar College of Music. He then moved to India, and spent a number of years learning tabla under the late Ustad Shaik Dawood Khan of Hyderabad. He has performed extensively on stage, TV, disk, CD, TV, and radio, in India, Europe and the United States. He is the author of numerous books and articles on the subject of Indian music including *Introduction to Tabla*, *Elementary North Indian Vocal*, *Fundamentals of Tabla*, *Manufacture and Repair of Tabla*, *Focus on the Kaidas of Tabla*, *Learning the Tabla* (Mel Bay MB99062M) and *Learning the Sitar* (Mel Bay MB20870M). His articles have appeared in "Modern Drummer," "Percussive Notes" and numerous other journals. He is currently active in the "Music Beyond Borders" collective at KPFT Houston. In 2009 he and his wife were designated as "Cultural Jewels of India" by the Indian Cultural Centre.

email - david@chandrakantha.com

Chandrakantha Courtney is a well known vocalist in the Indian community, both in the United State and Asia. She was formerly an artist in All India Radio of Vijaywada and Hyderabad. She has given music for several films, disks, cassettes, and countless radio and TV performances. She has performed extensively in India, South Africa, Malaysia, Singapore, Germany and the US. She is an artist with Young Audiences, Although she is mainly known as a vocalist, she received training in sitar under Dr. Sanjay Kingi and Atmaram Rao of Hyderabad. She is the coauthor of a book *Elementary North Indian Vocal* and also a contributor to *Learning the Tabla* (MB99062M) and *Learning the Sitar* (MB20870M). She was awarded "Artist of the Year" by Asian Women, and along with her husband, she was given an award of recognition for outstanding contributions to the arts by the American Telugu Association. In 2009, along with her husband, she was designated as being a "Cultural Jewel of India" by the Indian Cultural Centre.

email - chandra@chandrakantha.com

ABOUT THIS BOOK

Learning the Tabla Vol. 2

by David Courtney

The Indian tabla is a difficult pair of hand drums, but by no means should it be considered inaccessible. For those who have gone through the introductory Learning the Tabla, this book/audio is an ideal next step. It contains much new material which is appropriate for an intermediate level student. This series introduces us to new material, concepts, and techniques. Such material includes a discussion of the complementary nature of tabla bols/technique. It also introduces us to new compositional forms such as mukhada, rela, laggi, paran, gat, tihai, and chakradar. There is an introduction to the concept of transitional bols and techniques. This set also expands upon material that was introduced in the first set by giving new tals, and their thekas, as well as a more advanced kaida. There is also a discussion of the ancient barrel drum known as the pakhawaj and a discussion of pakhawaj material that can be played on the tabla. Includes access to online audio.

Toll Free 1-800-8-MEL BAY (1-800-863-5229)
Fax (636) 257-5062
email@melbay.com

www.MELBAY.com

MB20871M
$19.99 USD

$19.99

ISBN 978-078-668-619-3

51999

9 780786 686193